INCREDIBLE INDIANS
75 PEOPLE
WHO SHAPED MODERN INDIA

First published in India in 2022 by HarperCollins *Children's Books*
This edition published in 2025 by HarperCollins *Children's Books*
An imprint of HarperCollins *Publishers*
Building no 10, Tower A, 4th floor, DLF Cyber City,
Phase II, Gurugram 122002, India

www.harpercollins.co.in

2 4 6 8 10 9 7 5 3 1

Text © Ashwitha Jayakumar 2022, 2025
Illustrations © HarperCollins *Publishers* India 2022, 2025

P-ISBN: 978-93-6569-089-7
E-ISBN: 978-93-5489-264-6

Ashwitha Jayakumar asserts the moral right to be identified as the author of this work.

The views and opinions expressed in this book are the author's own and the facts are as reported by him/her, and the publishers are not in any way liable for the same.

While every effort has been made to ensure the accuracy of the facts presented in the book, the publishers are not liable for any inadvertent errors that might have crept in.

All rights reserved. No part of this publication may be reproduced, stored in a retrieval system, or transmitted, in any form or by any means, electronic, mechanical, photocopying, recording or otherwise, without the prior permission of the publishers.

Cover and inside design: Sergio Mario Studio
Typeset in Cormorant Garamond 11pt/ 14
by Sergio Mario Studio

Printed and bound at
Thomson Press (India) Ltd

This book is produced from independently certified FSC® paper
to ensure responsible forest management.

INCREDIBLE INDIANS
75 PEOPLE
WHO SHAPED MODERN INDIA

Ashwitha Jayakumar

Illustrated by
Sergio Mario Studio

HARPERCOLLINS
CHILDREN'S BOOKS

CONTENTS

1 FREEDOM SEEKERS
Mohandas Karamchand Gandhi — 12-13
Subhas Chandra Bose — 14-15
Jayaprakash Narayan, Jivatram Bhagwandas Kripalani, Rajendra Prasad — 16-17

2 CONSTITUTION MAKERS
Bhimrao Ramji 'Babasaheb' Ambedkar — 20-21
Qudsia Aizaz Rasul, Dakshayani Velayudhan — 22-23
Benegal Narsing Rau, Alladi Krishnaswamy Iyer, Hansa Mehta, Jaipal Singh Munda — 24-25

3 SHAPERS OF THE NATION
Vallabhbhai Patel — 28-29
Vappala Pangunni Menon — 30-31
Tanguturi Prakasam Pantulu, Shankarrao Deo, P Shilu Ao, Laldenga — 32-33

4 FEMALE PIONEERS
Amrit Kaur — 36-37
Muthulakshmi Reddy, Ammu Swaminathan — 38-39
Anna Chandy, EK Janaki Ammal, Vijaya Lakshmi Pandit — 40-41

5 SOLDIERS AND SPYMASTERS
Kodandera Subayya Thimayya — 44-45
Ram Dass Katari, Subroto Mukerjee — 46-47
Kodandera Madappa Cariappa, SHFJ Manekshaw, Rameshwar Nath Kao — 48-49

6 A DIFFERENT KIND OF POLITICS
Elamkulam Manakkal Sankaran Namboodiripad — 52-53
Conjeevaram Natarajan Annadurai — 54-55
Syama Prasad Mookerjee, Ram Manohar Lohia, Jyoti Basu, Kanshi Ram — 56-57

7 INSTITUTION BUILDERS
Abul Kalam Mohiuddin Ahmed — 60-61
Monkombu Sambasivan Swaminathan — 62-63
Vikram Sarabhai — 64-65
Homi J Bhabha, Prasanta Chandra Mahalanobis, Verghese Kurien — 66-67

8 — TITANS OF INDUSTRY
Ghanshyam Das Birla — 70-71
Jehangir Ratanji Dadabhoy Tata — 72-73
Jamnalal Bajaj, Ambalal Sarabhai, Khwaja Abdul Hamied — 74-75

9 — LEADERS OF THE NATION
Jawaharlal Nehru — 78-79
Indira Priyadarshini Gandhi — 80-81
Morarji Desai, Pamulaparti Venkata Narasimha Rao, Atal Bihari Vajpayee — 82-83

10 — GREEN WARRIORS
Salim Moizuddin Abdul Ali — 86-87
Gaura Devi, Kinkri Devi — 88-89
Chandi Prasad Bhatt, Sunderlal Bahuguna, Fateh Singh Rathore, Medha Patkar — 90-91

11 — RECLAIMING ART AND CULTURE
Kamaladevi Chattopadhyay — 94-95
Kapila Vatsyayan, Bal Krishen Thapar — 96-97
Bismillah Khan, Jagdish Swaminathan, MS Subbulakshmi — 98-99

12 — LITERARY MARVELS
Mulk Raj Anand — 102-103
Sarojini Naidu — 104-105
Rasipuram Krishnaswami Narayan, Ismat Chughtai, Mahasweta Devi — 106-107

13 — IN PURSUIT OF SOCIAL JUSTICE
Murlidhar Devidas 'Baba' Amte — 110-111
Ela Bhatt, Mabelle and Rajanikant Arole, Suniti Solomon — 112-113

14 — OTHER INCREDIBLE INDIANS — 114-121

FOREWORD

Marching on
Tushar A Gandhi is the great-grandson of Mahatma Gandhi. In March 2005, he led the seventy-fifth anniversary re-enactment of the Dandi March.

People and their deeds make a nation, not a land mass. Incredible people and their incredible deeds make an incredible nation. We take pride in calling our nation incredible. We must learn about the people who through the sheer dint of their efforts, dreams, courage, indomitable spirit, perseverance, integrity and their never-give-up spirit laid the solid foundation of our nation. These people helped build the incredible institutions that have stood the test of time and continue to be institutions of excellence which in turn make the nation incredible.

Incredible Indians: 75 People Who Shaped Modern India is a homage to some of the people who fought against all odds, surmounted various obstacles and triumphed through their achievements and sacrifices. Behind these seventy-five, there are hundreds, thousands and millions who silently helped these titans achieve their goals and realize their dreams. Nation-building could be compared to a war; even though the victory garland is for the triumphant general, every soldier who fights the battle contributes to the win. Nation-building, too, needs hundreds of thousands of unsung workers who deserve our appreciation. Today, when there is a dearth of living icons who inspire, the lives of these seventy-five iconic Indians need to be highlighted and celebrated. Our present and future generations must read these incredible stories, learn from them and be inspired by them. What one must understand is that behind each of these profiles is the determination and courage of these people to overcome adversity. APJ Abdul Kalam studied under street lanterns and went on to become India's Missile Man.

While in jail for fighting for India's freedom, Abul Kalam Azad did not succumb to adversity and used the opportunity to educate and enlighten himself to become India's first minister of education.

In the early part of his life, Mohandas Gandhi failed at almost everything he tried, be it his education, profession or his family life. But when push came to shove he did not give up and fought back courageously, learnt from his failures and turned them into his strengths. The rest as they say is history.

Although, eventually, we won freedom because of the non-violent freedom movement, the revolutionaries made a handsome contribution to the nationalist movement and its ultimate success. The Azad Hind Fauj was defeated in Imphal, but the war they waged was a major influence on our eventual freedom.

Sunderlal Bahuguna, with his Chipko Movement, spearheaded the environment protection and conservation movement at a time when not many were concerned about the plunder of natural resources and its adverse effects. Arunachalam Muruganantham, the Padman of India, in his zeal to provide his wife with hygienic and affordable sanitary pads, brought about a revolution for rural women by devising the technology to make affordable sanitary pads. SEWA has created a thriving bank for rural entrepreneurs; Sonam Wangchuk has brought about a knowledge and lifestyle revolution for the people of Ladakh and beyond through his scientific breakthroughs and inventions. Educator Anand Kumar, through his Super-30 coaching programme, has enabled severely underprivileged children to achieve their potential and make their dreams come true.

Incredible individuals who won glory for the nation, along with ordinary citizens who do their duty each day, need to be celebrated. Incredibles like the 'Flying Sikh' Milkha Singh, PT Usha, hockey legend Dhyan Chand, tennis great Ramanathan Krishnan, spin maestro Bishan Singh Bedi, king of the shuttlecock Prakash Padukone and chess grandmaster Viswanathan Anand have made the nation proud.

This book commemorates the lives of seventy-five such Indians who can be considered the builders of modern India. Being a living entity, a nation's future generations must step up and learn from the lives of their incredible ancestors. The extraordinary deeds of these ordinary Indians made an incredible nation. As we celebrate the seventy-fifth anniversary of our Independence, let us acknowledge these Indians and dedicate ourselves to emulate their deeds and do our bit to make India even more incredible!
Vande Mataram!

Tushar A Gandhi

AUTHOR'S NOTE

When I was first approached to write this book, the idea was that it would feature seventy-five 'makers of modern India' in order to commemorate India's seventy-fifth year of independence. But before I could dive into research, I had to answer a few questions for myself, starting with 'what is modern India'? And who counts as one of its 'makers'?

In answer to the first question, I took modern India to mean the independent nation-state of India that came into being on 15 August 1947 after decades of nationalist struggle against British colonial rule.

Next, I had to identify who the 'makers' of this modern India were. I was struck by the fact that although the subcontinent had a history going back thousands of years, the democratic nation that was created at Independence was an entirely new thing. It was an idea that brought together (for the first time) a bewildering variety of people with very different experiences into a single political unit. India's 'makers', therefore, were the people who helped shape the former colony into a cohesive and independent nation, and gave it a new identity in terms of its politics, borders, culture, society and economy.

But I immediately ran into difficulties because of the sheer number of people who were involved in nation-building. To me, it seemed like modern India would not be what it is without the contributions of the hundreds, even thousands of people who built and ran institutions, dictated government policy and pushed for social reform. But trying to include all or even most of them would have resulted in a very long, very thick book that would probably have taken me decades to complete.

So I slowly chipped away at the list to cut it down, excluding some people because their work did not fall within the time period of the book (roughly the 1920s to 2000) and some because there just wasn't enough verifiable information available. I also excluded people in order to balance the numbers between those who continue to be celebrated and those who, through no fault of their own, have largely been forgotten. And finally, in order to make the list as widely representative as possible, I preferentially included as many people as I could from traditionally marginalized communities.

The final and perhaps hardest task was trying to compress a person's whole life and work into a few hundred words. Every one of the people you will read about seem to have packed three lifetimes' worth of living into one. This made the process of researching and writing about them both time-consuming and difficult, for the more I learned, the more I wanted to say about each person. I found myself despairing over how I could possibly to do them justice within the limited space available. How could I encapsulate their rich, complex lives and legacies in so few words?

Inevitably, I have had to leave a lot out.

And so, at last, I arrived at a list of seventy-five individuals who shaped modern India. Some of them, such as MK Gandhi or Jawaharlal Nehru, continue to be idolized or seen as heroic figures. Others, such as Muthulakshmi Reddy or Jayaprakash Narayan, created a sensation when they were alive, but are less well-known today. And still others, like Gaura Devi are rarely ever mentioned. I have deliberately tried to steer clear of presenting people as heroes or villains, which is all too often the manner in which the makers of modern India are spoken of. Instead, I have tried to write as impartially as possible about people who, in a variety of ways and for better or for worse, played a part in shaping the history and progress of the modern Indian nation. I find them all endlessly fascinating. I hope you will too.

To Tina Narang and Medha Gupta at HarperCollins, thank you so much for giving me the space and time to make this book what it is and for helping to make it better. I also owe thanks to Priyal, who took my drab blocks of text and transformed them into interesting pages punctuated with photographs and vivid illustrations.

To the many people who patiently looked over my lists of names, read drafts, made insightful comments, gave me reading recommendations and pointed out errors, both large and small—you should know I couldn't have done this without your help. I am especially grateful to Shalini Agrawal, who proofread the entire book and provided valuable feedback.

I am also grateful to the many historians and biographers who have written on modern India. Reading their work helped me discover just how complex and interesting modern Indian history can be.

And finally, to my mum, grandma, and brother, my friends and my partner, who have all had to compete with India's makers for my attention over the last two years: thank you for listening to all my stories.

Ashwitha Jayakumar

To better reflect the lived reality of the people in the book, I have largely used the names of Indian cities and states as they would have known them. Where appropriate, present-day names are given in parentheses, and occasional use is made of present-day names for the sake of convenience where space is scarce.

1
FREEDOM SEEKERS

> "It is a fateful moment for us in India, for all Asia and for the world. A new star rises, the star of freedom in the east, a new hope comes into being, a vision long cherished materialises. May the star never set and that hope never be betrayed!"
>
> *Jawaharlal Nehru, 1947*

The English first arrived on the subcontinent as traders in the 1600s. At the time, India was a vastly wealthy trading giant with international connections and a diversity of people, cultures, languages and religions. Over the next two hundred years, the English turned from traders into colonial masters and established a whole system of government to achieve their primary goal: the transfer of India's wealth to their own faraway country. Indian lives came to be regulated by English laws implemented by English administrators, who were implicitly considered more civilized than those they ruled over. But as Indians across the subcontinent became empowered by education in the twentieth century, they began to challenge Britain's right to rule.

The Indian National Congress came into being in 1885, marking the beginning of a sustained effort, by the Congress and others, to demand representation in government, equality under the law and, later on, full independence for Indians. In different ways and at different times, scores of Indians wrote, argued, protested, lobbied, assassinated, marched, went to prison and died for their belief in India's right to be an independent nation. In a way, every one of them helped build modern India.

This section focuses on five key figures within the movement for independence, each of whom had strong views on how India could become independent and what that independent nation should be like.

MOHANDAS KARAMCHAND GANDHI
1869–1948

The making of the Mahatma

Mohandas Karamchand Gandhi was the son of Karamchand Gandhi, the dewan of the princely state of Porbandar, and Putlibai. Young Mohandas travelled to London at eighteen to study law. In 1893, now a qualified lawyer, he accepted a job that took him to the British colony of Natal, South Africa. There, he was struck by the blatant racial discrimination that Indian workers were subjected to. Gandhi himself was famously thrown out of a first-class train carriage because it was meant for whites only. Determined to fight back, he threw himself into campaigning for Indians' rights by drafting petitions, writing newspaper articles and organizing strikes. Over the course of twenty years, he established a reputation for himself as a principled and committed campaigner for freedom both in South Africa and back home.

A new path to freedom

In 1915, Gandhi returned to India. At the time, the nationalist Congress was divided on whether to pursue their goals through violent resistance or through cooperation with the British. Gandhi suggested a third path, one defined by non-violent non-cooperation. And so, from 1920 onwards, Indians all over the country were encouraged to boycott British-made goods as well as British-run schools, colleges, jobs and courts. Also, the Congress had until then been dominated by the educated elite. Gandhi encouraged people from a variety of castes, classes and backgrounds to participate in the nationalist movement. From 1934, Gandhi also asked people to engage in civil disobedience, which involved not paying taxes and not following unfair British laws, in order to show the British that Indians would not accept a government biased against them.

Gandhian ideals

After his return, Gandhi travelled across India, and soon realized that the British were only one of many oppressive forces at work across the land—untouchability, religious conflict, poverty and a lack

SATYAGRAHA OR 'TRUTH FORCE'

Gandhi first came up with and practised the idea of satyagraha, a way of protesting without violence and living the truth of one's beliefs, in South Africa. This idea would eventually change the course of the Indian independence movement.

of education were all issues that needed to be dealt with in order for Indians to live truly free lives. So he launched a programme of progressive social change, and encouraged people to lead simpler lives and to learn to create useful things with their hands. He promoted good sanitation, led campaigns against caste- and gender-based discriminatory practices, and tried to get India's many religious and social groups to work together. From industrialists and farmers to princesses and poets, the ideas he articulated brought him thousands of devoted followers.

> "AFTER I AM GONE, NO SINGLE PERSON WILL BE ABLE COMPLETELY TO REPRESENT ME…BUT A LITTLE BIT OF ME WILL LIVE IN MANY OF YOU."

Gandhi's methods of non-violent protest influenced generations of freedom fighters and activists all over the world. US civil rights activist Martin Luther King Jr, South African anti-apartheid activist (and later president) Nelson Mandela, as well as the Dalai Lama, the exiled Tibetan spiritual leader, all count him among their influences.

Death and legacy

In 1947, British India was partitioned into India and Pakistan. This forced many thousands of Hindus, Muslims and Sikhs to leave their homes to make new lives far away. It also led to tremendous communal violence in which many thousands died. A horrified Gandhi, now in his seventies, travelled across the country pleading with people to lay down their arms and stop fighting. Although revered by millions, there were some who disagreed with Gandhi's ideas and disapproved of his methods. For instance, some Muslims, including Mohammed Ali Jinnah, believed that Gandhi put the interests of Hindus first, while Hindu nationalists believed Gandhi had more sympathy for Muslims than for Hindus. This latter belief was to prove deadly: on 30 January 1948, a Hindu nationalist named Nathuram Godse assassinated Gandhi in New Delhi. His death so soon after the achievement of independence was mourned by millions, both in India and in the world at large. Today, Gandhi's beliefs and legacy are questioned by some. But, despite his flaws, there can be no doubt that he had an immense and lasting impact on his nation—and the world.

SUBHAS CHANDRA BOSE
1897–1945

The desire to serve

Subhas Chandra Bose was the son of Janakinath Bose, a successful Calcutta (now Kolkata) lawyer, and Prabhabati. Bose spent a sheltered childhood in Orissa (now Odisha), a time in which he was largely unaware of the politics of British India. It was only when he moved to Calcutta to study philosophy that he was struck by the inequality and discrimination rampant in colonial India.

> "IF WE WANT TO MAKE INDIA REALLY GREAT WE MUST BUILD UP A POLITICAL DEMOCRACY ON THE PEDESTAL OF A DEMOCRATIC SOCIETY."

Freedom for everyone

In the late 1920s and the 1930s, the British arrested Bose and jailed him several times. During one stint in jail, his health grew so poor that the government offered to send him to Europe to recover, so long as he did not return to India. During this period, he came to believe that India needed modernization, industrialization and a strong military, and that socialism could change society for the better. Crucially, he did not agree with Gandhi's non-violent approach, as he felt that it was too slow and ineffective.

CALCUTTA TO CAMBRIDGE TO CONGRESS

Bose was accused of beating up a British professor and expelled from Presidency College in 1916. He subsequently went to Cambridge to take the Indian Civil Services exam. Despite having only a few months to prepare, he achieved a high rank. But the brilliant young man resigned from the prestigious appointment he received because he could not bring himself to serve the British Raj. Upon his return to India in 1921, Bose joined the Congress and participated in the non-cooperation movement, organizing protests and writing articles critical of the British.

Uneasy allies

In 1939, World War II broke out in Europe, with Britain fighting Germany, Italy and Japan. Bose thought Britain's enemies could be India's friends. So he disguised himself and made a daring escape out of India. He travelled to Berlin, where he hoped to convince Hitler and the Nazis to support India's struggle for independence (even though he personally disapproved of the Nazis' racist ideology). Receiving only limited support from them, in 1943 Bose decided to reach out to the Japanese for help, and embarked on a daredevil journey via submarine and airplane. Once back in Asia, he founded the Azad Hind Fauj (Indian National Army) and trained Indian soldiers and workers whom he convinced to join his cause.

Bose's strong belief in the equality of men and women led him to form the very first all-female regiment anywhere in the world. Named after the Rani of Jhansi, it was commanded by Lakshmi Sahgal.

AZAD HIND GOVERNMENT

Bose formed the Azad Hind government in October 1943 in Singapore. It had its own currency, court and army (the INA). The INA fought British Indian Army troops in Burma with the support of the Japanese, and even reached Kohima and Imphal in the north-east of India before suffering a crushing defeat.

The Renkoji temple in Tokyo is believed to be the final resting place of Bose's ashes.

A tragic end

When Bose's allies were defeated in World War II, he decided to travel to the Soviet Union (now Russia) for aid. Tragically, the plane he was on crashed in Taiwan. Not even fifty years old, Bose died, his dream of seeing an independent India unrealized. People refused to believe that a fearless and dynamic leader like Bose could have met such an untimely end. Rumours about his survival continued for decades, a testament to his enduring popularity. According to both the Indian and Japanese governments, none of these have any truth to them.

FROM PROTEST TO POLITICS

Many who participated in India's freedom struggle went on to have an impact on how the country was run after 1947. With their strong views and readiness to speak up for what they believed in, the three men below helped shape politics, power and protests in modern India.

JAYAPRAKASH NARAYAN
1902–1979

"THOSE WHO OCCUPY HIGH PLACES IN SOCIETY—IN POLITICS, BUSINESS, THE PROFESSIONS—BEAR THE HEAVY RESPONSIBILITY OF LEADING THE PEOPLE BY PERSONAL EXAMPLE."

Jayaprakash Narayan was a socialist, an admirer of Gandhi, and a prominent figure in the nationalist movement. He quit politics in 1954 to work more directly for the welfare of the poor. A persuasive public speaker, he spoke out against political and bureaucratic corruption during the Indira Gandhi regime, and was imprisoned for leading a hugely popular resistance movement against her government. He subsequently helped form the Janata Party, which defeated the Congress in the 1977 elections and formed the first ever non-Congress government since Independence.

> **SOCIALISM**
>
> Socialism is a way of organizing people and resources so that the gap between the rich and the poor is very small or non-existent. In a socialist country, everyone would cooperate and share resources, with the government helping to ensure this.

JIVATRAM BHAGWANDAS KRIPALANI
1888–1982

JB Kripalani studied history and economics in Pune before becoming a teacher. He joined the Congress in the 1920s and was an ardent follower of Gandhi. Always a man who spoke his mind, Kripalani left the Congress in 1951, after several years of disagreements with the party's leadership. Like Gandhi, he felt strongly that India's future lay in its villages. He founded the Kisan Mazdoor Praja Party, hoping to strengthen local government and work towards improving the lives of India's poor. Kripalani was known for his strong principles and uncompromising criticism of his colleagues. Along with Jayaprakash Narayan, he led the resistance against Indira Gandhi's government, also serving time in prison for it.

RAJENDRA PRASAD
1884–1963

"IN OUR COUNTRY, PARTICULARLY, IT IS VERY NECESSARY THAT EACH OF US SHOULD REALISE THAT THE BEST COURSE IS TO ACT WITH A SENSE OF RESPECT AND EQUALITY TOWARDS EVERY COMMUNITY AND CREED."

Viceroy House became Rashtrapati Bhavan after 1947 and is the president's official residence. The lovely Mughal Gardens that are part of it were opened to the public for the first time under Prasad and continue to be a popular attraction.

Rajendra Prasad was a young lawyer from Bihar who joined the ranks of Gandhi's followers soon after the latter's return to India. Brought up in an orthodox upper-caste home, he nonetheless learned to shed his prejudices and, with Gandhi, campaigned against untouchability. He was a key member of the Congress, and served as President of the Constituent Assembly. In this role, he mediated between different groups with opposing views, and earned praise for his patience and impartiality. He was subsequently appointed the first president of India. During his twelve years in office, the conflicts that arose, especially between him and the prime minister, helped shape the role of the president and determine the limits of their powers.

2
CONSTITUTION MAKERS

"It is essential for any constitution... to make all the citizens realize... that there will be cultural autonomy; that nobody will be suppressed; that it will be a constitution which will be democratic in the true sense of the term, where, from political freedom, we will march on to economic freedom and equity."

— Sarvepalli Radhakrishnan, 1946

A constitution is a set of rules according to which a nation is organized and governed. It is the basis of a country's laws and defines the powers and duties of the government, as well as citizens' rights and duties. Indians had demanded the right to create their own constitution for decades, but it was only in 1946 that a Constituent Assembly first gathered to undertake this mammoth task. Made up of over 300 individuals, the Assembly met for 11 sessions that spanned 165 days. The product of their labours was the document that laid the foundations of the modern Indian state.

The Assembly was chosen via indirect election and nomination, and committees were appointed to research and present reports on specific issues, which were then thoroughly discussed. A Drafting Committee was nominated and tasked with preparing a draft constitution, which was then put up for further discussion. The members of the Assembly were a reasonably diverse group (although dominated by upper-caste Hindu men from the Congress, the Constituent Assembly included fifteen women and representatives from other religious groups), with a variety of ideologies, beliefs and perspectives. This made for lively debates on a wide range of issues, such as what the official language of India should be, whether there should be reservations for historically disadvantaged communities and what rights could be granted to all citizens.

India's constitution-making process was among the first of its kind in the world. The many hours the Assembly spent resulted in a progressive, ambitious and egalitarian document. This section features a few of the remarkable people who helped create it.

BHIMRAO RAMJI 'BABASAHEB' AMBEDKAR
1891–1956

The making of the scholar

Ambedkar was the fourteenth child of Ramji Sakpal, an officer in the British Indian army, and Bhimabai. The family belonged to the Mahar caste, which was considered 'untouchable' in the Hindu caste system. Discrimination was a near-constant in Ambedkar's life from a very young age. At school, he was not allowed to sit near his classmates or touch the common drinking water tap they used. But his fierce intelligence earned him scholarships that took him first to Bombay (now Mumbai), then to Columbia University in New York and finally to the London School of Economics. By the time he returned to India for good in 1923, he was one of the best educated men in the country. Yet, no matter how well-educated or well-dressed he became, Ambedkar continued to be viciously discriminated against by his countrymen.

> Separate electorates were introduced by the British, supposedly as a way to ensure that minorities (like Muslims) would be fairly represented in government. A certain number of seats were reserved for minority candidates, and only voters belonging to those communities were allowed to vote for them.

A voracious reader, Ambedkar bought more than 2,000 books on a variety of subjects from second-hand bookstores in the US. Tragically, the ship carrying his books home in 1917 was sunk by a German torpedo strike.

Fighting against the caste system

Ambedkar would wage a lifelong battle against caste-based and gender-based prejudice. He was outspoken and uncompromising in calling out injustice and saw the caste system as an entrenched evil that needed to be destroyed. He also believed that the 'Depressed Classes' (the term used then; the preferred term today is Dalit) had to fight for their own rights rather than rely on upper-caste Hindus to initiate reforms. He established several organizations, began his own political parties, and led campaigns to educate Dalits about their rights. He also tried to work with the British to secure political representation for the 'lower' castes. When Gandhi and the Congress did not agree to his demand for separate electorates for Dalits, Ambedkar began to doubt the upper-caste dominated Congress's commitment to fighting caste prejudice.

Framing the Constitution

Ambedkar believed that the law and government would play an important role in reforming society and that a country could only progress economically when it also progressed socially. Being part of the Constituent Assembly thus afforded him an important opportunity to lay the foundation for this social progress: he helped frame a constitution that would grant equal rights to all of India's citizens, protect the marginalized and work towards social justice. As Chairman of the Drafting Committee, he took on the arduous task of putting the Constitution together. In this role, he had to explain the committee's views, and defend how and why a sentence or a clause was written in a certain way.

In 1927, Ambedkar marched with 'untouchables' in the town of Mahad, Maharashtra, and drank water from a tank they had been denied access to by upper-caste Hindus. The latter, believing the water was now polluted, conducted a purification ritual that involved the addition of curd, cow dung, cow urine and milk to the water.

> "INDEPENDENCE IS NO DOUBT A MATTER OF JOY. BUT LET US NOT FORGET THAT THIS INDEPENDENCE HAS THROWN ON US GREAT RESPONSIBILITIES. BY INDEPENDENCE, WE HAVE LOST THE EXCUSE OF BLAMING THE BRITISH FOR ANYTHING GOING WRONG. IF HEREAFTER THINGS GO WRONG, WE WILL HAVE NOBODY TO BLAME EXCEPT OURSELVES."

The Hindu Code Bill

Ambedkar's other major project was the controversial Hindu Code Bill, which sought to create laws that would give Hindu women the same rights as Hindu men. Conservative Hindu groups, such as the Hindu Mahasabha, and members of the Congress like Rajendra Prasad opposed the bill. When even a watered-down version couldn't be passed, Ambedkar resigned as law minister in 1951. The bill was eventually split into parts, debated and passed between 1952 and 1956, although some of its original provisions were diluted. However, the fact that it was possible at all was due to Ambedkar's unwavering commitment to equality.

Ambedkar died in 1956 at the age of sixty-six, having made enormous contributions to both his community and country in his lifetime. His life and work continue to inspire contemporary anti-caste movements.

QUDSIA AIZAZ RASUL
1908–2001

"...THE WOMEN OF INDIA ARE HAPPY TO STEP INTO THEIR RIGHTFUL HERITAGE OF COMPLETE EQUALITY WITH MEN..."

From purdah to Parliament

Qudsia Aizaz Rasul was born into a junior branch of the ruling family of Malerkotla. She grew up in a wealthy household, where her father's involvement in politics nurtured her own interest in public service. However, it was only after her marriage to a landowner named Nawab Aizaz Rasul in 1929 that she began to actively take part in politics. She won a seat on the United Provinces (now Uttar Pradesh) Legislative Council in 1937. Despite opposition from orthodox men in the region, Rasul was a popular politician who was re-elected several times.

After being elected to public office, Rasul took the then-controversial decision to give up purdah. This practice, followed by both Hindu and Muslim women in north India, forced women to remain sequestered from people outside their families and thus denied many the opportunity to get an education or move freely in society.

Aizaz Rasul was president of the Indian Women's Hockey Federation for over fifteen years and worked hard to help girls in India participate in sports without fear of discrimination.

The Begum's life and legacy

Rasul was elected to the Constituent Assembly, where she was a vocal participant in the debates. Notably, she helped convince other Muslim members to agree to joint electorates after Independence, and argued in favour of children receiving an education in their mother tongues. She was also a member of the All India Women's Conference (like many of the women in this book) and believed women should have equal rights, which she advocated throughout her time in politics. Rasul continued to serve in government after 1947 as a member of the Rajya Sabha and later as a member of the Uttar Pradesh Legislative Assembly.

DAKSHAYANI VELAYUDHAN
1912–1978

An unusual family

Dakshayani Velayudhan was born into a Dalit family in present-day Kerala. At the time, social rules dictated every aspect of the lives of so-called lower-caste individuals, from the kind of clothes they could wear, to where they could live, and how they could earn a living. They were also frequently denied access to education. But Velayudhan was born to progressive parents in a region that had a history of strong anti-caste movements. Her own family had resisted discrimination from those higher up in the caste hierarchy. With their support, she became the first scheduled-caste woman to receive a bachelor's degree.

> Dakshayani's wedding to Dalit leader R Velayudhan was performed by a priest suffering from leprosy. Leprosy is an infectious disease that can be cured but can cause terrible disfigurement. Because of this, people who suffer from it have historically been ostracized.

"THE WORKING OF THE CONSTITUTION WILL DEPEND UPON HOW THE PEOPLE WILL CONDUCT THEMSELVES IN THE FUTURE, NOT ON THE ACTUAL EXECUTION OF THE LAW. SO I HOPE THAT IN COURSE OF TIME THERE WILL NOT BE SUCH A COMMUNITY KNOWN AS UNTOUCHABLES..."

A driven woman

Dakshayani admired Gandhi, and was also inspired by BR Ambedkar's anti-caste politics. She, too, became involved in campaigning against untouchability. At the age of thirty-four, she joined the Constituent Assembly as its youngest member. In the Assembly debates, she was vocal about the need to make untouchability illegal, arguing that it was the duty of the government to educate people and help abolish caste. In 1977, she founded the Mahila Jagriti Parishad to help Dalit women gain access to education and vocational training.

At college, Dakshayani had to fight to be treated the same way as her classmates. An upper-caste teacher would not allow her to stand near enough to observe experiments for fear that her low-caste status would be 'polluting'.

A DIVERSE GROUP

An effort was made to include as many capable people as possible in the constitution-making process, including the four individuals on these pages.

BENEGAL NARSING RAU
1887–1953

"A CONSTITUTION IS ONLY A MEANS TO AN END...WHEN BY WORKING TOGETHER AS A TEAM, VARIOUS PARTIES REALIZE THAT THE ENDS ARE COMMON, THERE WILL BE LITTLE DIFFICULTY IN AGREEING UPON THE MEANS."

Born in present-day Karnataka, **BN Rau** was a brilliant student who successfully qualified for a position in the Indian Civil Service. Renowned for his knowledge of constitutional law, Rau was appointed Constitutional Advisor to the Drafting Committee in 1946. He travelled across the world to study other countries' constitutions and consult with local lawyers and judges on constitutional issues. Based on his research, he prepared an entire draft constitution that deeply influenced the thinking and approach of the Assembly. Ambedkar himself stated that at least part of the credit for the framing of the Constitution must go to Rau (who was not actually a member of the Assembly himself).

Much of the day-to-day administration of British India was undertaken by Indian Civil Service men. A post in the ICS brought influence and perks, and was much sought after. From 1853, anyone who could pass the exams could secure a post—including Indians. However, since one had to travel to England to take these exams, only the wealthiest Indians could aspire to this.

ALLADI KRISHNASWAMI IYER
1883–1953

Born in present-day Andhra Pradesh, **AK Iyer** was a successful and well-regarded lawyer who served as Advocate General of Madras State for many years. He was considered by his peers to be one of the most successful lawyers of his generation. Although not a politician, his reputation as a legal expert and his extensive knowledge of both Indian and foreign law made him a valuable asset to the Constituent Assembly. He was part of nine committees, including the ones on fundamental rights and the government's powers as well as the Drafting Committee. His contributions included defining who would be considered a citizen of India and highlighting the differences between the fundamental rights and the directive principles.

HANSA JIVRAJ MEHTA
1897–1995

Hansa Mehta was born into a liberal Gujarati family. While studying in England, she became acquainted with several Congress leaders and was inspired to join the freedom struggle. Mehta's life was marked by brave choices: she married a man outside her caste; she organized anti-colonial protests and served three terms in prison. A long-time advocate of equal rights for women, including in matters like inheritance and divorce, Mehta was keen to ensure that women's rights were enshrined in the Constitution.

JAIPAL SINGH MUNDA
1903–1970

Jaipal Singh Munda belonged to the Munda tribe, whose members live in the present-day states of Jharkhand, Odisha and West Bengal. He studied economics at the University of Oxford, and was a talented hockey player who captained the gold-medal-winning Indian field hockey team at the 1928 Summer Olympics. After his return to India in the 1930s, he joined the Adivasi movement, which sought to represent India's marginalized tribal communities. Singh was elected to the Constituent Assembly as an independent candidate. A tireless activist for tribal rights, he highlighted their lack of representation in government and the extreme exploitation they had faced for centuries. For his efforts, he earned the title 'marang gomke' or 'great leader' among the people he represented.

3
SHAPERS OF THE NATION

> "To have dissolved 554 States by integrating them into the pattern of the Republic; to have brought about order out of the nightmare of chaos whence we started... should steel us on to the attainment of equal success in other spheres. For the first time, India has become an integrated whole in the real sense of the term..."
>
> VP Menon, 1956

India in 2024 consists of twenty-eight states and eight union territories, but this wasn't always the case. In fact, the subcontinent on the eve of Independence was divided into British India (the territory directly under British control), and over five hundred large, medium-sized and tiny princely states (Hyderabad, Jammu and Kashmir, and Mysore, for example, were all princely states). Their rulers had signed treaties with the British that gave the latter a degree of control over their kingdoms in exchange for riches or protection. And then there were parts of India that were ruled by other European countries, such as the Portuguese colonies of Goa, Daman and Diu, and the French colony of Pondicherry (now Puducherry). All of these had to somehow be knitted together into a nation.

India's political shape has continued to shift and change after 1947. Indians have always been a heterogeneous group, speaking hundreds of different languages, belonging to a vast number of communities, castes, tribes and faiths, and following a bewildering diversity of customs, traditions and practices. Different groups and communities fought to be seen and heard in the new nation, with language, culture, religion and customs becoming flashpoints for conflict. This led to power struggles between the state and its people. In some cases, these conflicts have continued to the present day.

In this section, you will read about a few individuals whose actions impacted the very shape of the Indian nation—from those who tried to glue the different pieces of British and princely India together into a unified country, to those who believed, for a time, that some of those pieces would be better apart.

VALLABHBHAI PATEL
1875–1950

The young Vallabhbhai
Patel was one of six children of Jhaverbhai Patel and his wife Ladba. Unable to afford a university education, young Vallabhbhai relied on borrowed books and hard work to qualify as a District Pleader just two years after finishing school (a pleader was a very basic type of lawyer). At thirty-six, he travelled to England, after having saved enough to fulfil his dream of becoming a barrister. Upon his return, Patel, now an English-speaking man in European attire, focused his energies on raising his two young children, and building a reputation as a successful lawyer.

"FOR UNITY, WE MUST FORGET DIFFERENCES OF CASTE AND CREED AND REMEMBER THAT WE ARE ALL INDIANS, AND ALL EQUAL…ALL MUST HAVE EQUAL OPPORTUNITIES, EQUAL RIGHTS AND EQUAL RESPONSIBILITIES. THIS IS DIFFICULT FOR ACHIEVEMENT IN PRACTICE, BUT WE MUST CONTINUOUSLY STRIVE TOWARDS THAT END."

Joining the fight
After moving a couple of times, Patel and his family eventually settled in a town called Borsad in present-day Gujarat. Here, he became known for being methodical in the way he presented his cases and fierce in his pursuit of justice. It wasn't until Mohandas Gandhi entered Patel's world in 1917 that he decided to join the fight for freedom. Over the next three decades, Patel grew into an important and well-respected member of the Indian National Congress, with Gandhi coming to rely on his pragmatism, organizational skills and ability to accomplish what he set out to achieve. By the time the British agreed to leave India, Patel was a front runner to be the first prime minister of India, although he was eventually appointed home minister and deputy prime minister.

After he joined the independence movement, Patel gave up his previous fondness for European clothing and followed Gandhi in adopting a simple lifestyle.

PATEL AND NEHRU

The socialist, secular Nehru and the economically and socially conservative Patel often disagreed on key issues. Gandhi frequently had to make peace between them, for he believed that the new India needed both men in order to grow and flourish. In the end, Patel and Nehru grew to respect each other and worked closely together for many years.

The man of action

Patel's most enduring contribution to India was getting the hundreds of rulers of princely states to agree to be part of free India. All through early 1947, Patel held meetings with royals who had to decide whether to join India or Pakistan or remain independent once the British left. Along with VP Menon, Patel convinced, intimidated or cajoled ruler after ruler to sign a document that would officially make their kingdom part of India. By August, Patel had been astonishingly successful. The majority of the negotiations were concluded peacefully, but in a few cases, such as Junagadh and Hyderabad, Patel had to resort to a show of military force to get their rulers to comply.

Partition and Patel

During Partition, tensions were high and horrific violence broke out in many parts of the country, with people turning on each other in a frenzy of communal hatred. As home minister, Patel was at the forefront of trying to stop the violence and look after the refugees now pouring into India. Patel's actions and thoughts at the time have been criticized as being biased. However, he did not hold back from punishing Hindus and Sikhs who attacked Muslims (and vice versa), and personally visited several riot-prone parts of Delhi to ensure the safety of the city's Muslims. Patel died in 1950, just three years after India became free, but his impact lives on in the very shape of the country even today.

VAPPALA PANGUNNI MENON
1893–1965

Starting at the bottom
Menon was born into a large landed family in present-day Kerala. He had a mostly pleasant childhood that ended abruptly when, at the age of thirteen, he set fire to his school in anger after being penalized for poor attendance. He subsequently ran away from home, which was the start of a life that would take him all over India, from the Kolar gold mines in Karnataka to Bombay and Simla. He entered government service as a typist at the age of twenty-one, and quickly built up a reputation for thoroughness and excellence, which earned him a permanent position in the British Indian government.

Menon's government career almost ended before it had even begun. When he was at the station to buy a ticket to travel to Simla (the British Indian government's summer capital), he discovered that his wallet was missing. Fortunately, a kind stranger gave him ten rupees to buy a ticket.

VP Menon is believed to have had a photographic memory. He shared this trait with several famous people in history, including Leonardo da Vinci and Nikola Tesla.

"We shall overcome and success will be ours in the future. The future belongs to us."
Savitribai Phule, 1856

The majority of women in colonial India had little or no access to education, and hardly any say in when and whom they married. Women could not move about freely in public, and could not divorce or remarry if widowed. They also did not have the right to inherit wealth. In the nineteenth century, the British government in India, foreign missionaries and reformers like Rammohan Roy, Ishwar Chandra Vidyasagar, Mahadev Govind Ranade and Jyotirao Phule began to take steps towards social change and improving women's lives. Largely initiated by men for women, their reforms sought to address oppressive practices but were not always based on a belief in gender equality. Nonetheless, by the time the twentieth century and the nationalist movement began, there was a small number of elite, educated, outspoken women who were entering professions and government positions so far dominated by men.

Not everyone saw this as a good thing. Some of the early male nationalists believed that a woman's place was in the home, and thought letting women study or make their own choices were 'Western' ideas that had no place in India. But when Gandhi called for both men and women to participate in the fight for freedom, women across castes, classes and religious groups joined in the thousands. At the same time, women's organizations began to push for even more reforms and guarantees from both the British and the Congress. Ideas about the roles women could play changed drastically, and women themselves demanded equal rights. The women in this section and many more like them helped lay the foundations of a more gender-equal society, which India continues to strive for even today.

AMRIT KAUR
1889–1964

Childhood inspirations

Amrit Kaur was the only daughter of Rani Lady Harnam Singh and Raja Sir Harnam Singh of Kapurthala. Kaur's father supported the struggle for freedom and was acquainted with several members of the Congress. Kaur's early exposure to discussions on India's freedom sparked a lasting passion for social reform and the independence movement. She was particularly inspired by Gandhi, and even wrote to him in 1918 to express her desire to join him despite her parents' disapproval. He wrote back encouraging her to respect her parents' wishes. So it was only in 1930, after both her parents had died, that she travelled to his ashram and was able to fully involve herself in the fight for freedom.

> "MY IDEAL HAPPINESS…CONSISTS IN DOING GOOD ALWAYS, EVEN TO THOSE WHO DO EVIL TO US, IN LOVING OUR NEIGHBOURS AS OURSELVES AND DOING TO ALL MEN AS WE WOULD HAVE THEM TO US, IN BEING GENTLE, MERCIFUL AND FORGIVING, IN NEVER BOASTING BUT ALWAYS HUMBLY TRYING TO DO RIGHT IN EVERYTHING."

Fighting for equality

Before and during her involvement with the Congress, Kaur dedicated time and effort towards other causes, especially women's rights. She was a member (and later president) of the All India Women's Conference, and campaigned against child marriage and polygamy. She also lobbied for women to have access to education and the right to vote. As a member of the Constituent Assembly, she made significant contributions to the debates on fundamental rights and minority rights. Both Kaur and her fellow champion of women's rights, Hansa Mehta, were against reservations for women and voiced support for a secular uniform civil code, which they felt would eliminate discriminatory practices in the laws of India's many religious communities.

Amrit Kaur became a close associate of Gandhi's, and served as his secretary for sixteen years. She felt particularly strongly about his non-violent philosophy and worked with him on social welfare programmes.

A man on the inside

It was the infamous Jallianwala Bagh massacre in 1919 that first made Menon appreciate the complexity of his position: he was an ambitious Indian employee of the British government, but was also sympathetic to the idea of a free India. Menon was thus well-positioned to create change from within. He was involved in the drafting of new laws that granted Indians more political representation and power. He also advised at least three British viceroys on the implementation of these laws. Seen as capable and trustworthy, he was handpicked by Vallabhbhai Patel to aid him in the important task of integrating the princely states into India.

> **WHAT CAME BEFORE THE CONSTITUTION?**
>
> Before the Constitution of India was adopted, the Government of India Acts of 1919 and 1935 passed by the British acted as a sort of constitution for British India. These acts set out, among other things, how many Indians could be elected to governing bodies, what their powers would be and which Indians could vote in elections.

The consummate advisor

Menon is mainly remembered today for his work with Patel. But Menon made another lasting contribution during the tumultuous months before 15th August in helping to determine how and to whom power would be transferred when British rule ended. The first proposal made by Lord Mountbatten was that power should be transferred initially to provincial governments, which could then decide whether they wanted to group together, and stay in India or not. In theory, this could have led to the formation of a dozen or more 'countries' in the subcontinent. Menon helped formulate the alternative that was finally accepted: the British would hand over power to the governments of two new dominions, India and Pakistan.

Lord Louis Mountbatten was the last Viceroy of India. Menon worked closely with him as Constitutional Advisor and later as Secretary of the States Department to determine the shape of the country.

FORGING A NATION

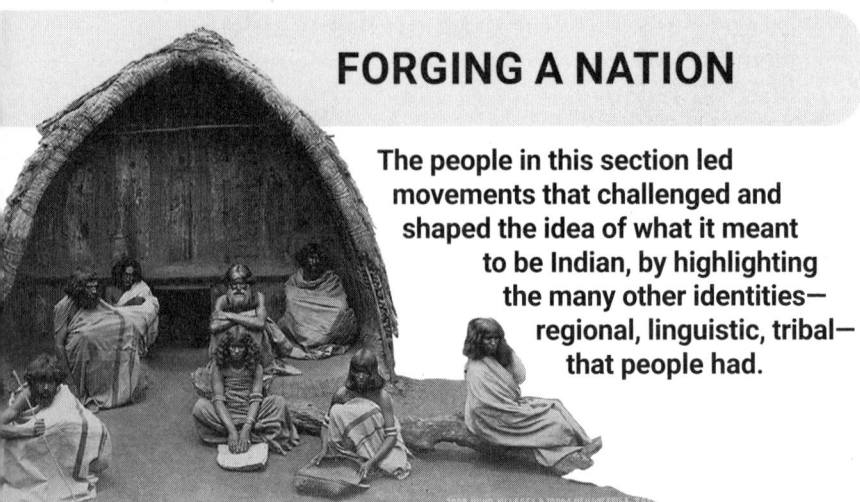

The people in this section led movements that challenged and shaped the idea of what it meant to be Indian, by highlighting the many other identities—regional, linguistic, tribal—that people had.

TANGUTURI PRAKASAM PANTULU
1872–1957

> "WHEN WE DEMAND SEPARATION WE DO NOT MEAN, AND WE CANNOT MEAN THAT WE CUT AWAY FROM OUR BRETHREN ALTOGETHER. SEPARATION IS ONLY FOR THE SAKE OF ADMINISTRATIVE CONVENIENCE AND DEVELOPMENT OF EACH AREA. ALL OTHER BONDS OF BUSINESS, FRIENDSHIP AND RELATIONSHIP REMAIN INTACT."

Tanguturi Prakasam Pantulu was a lawyer and a member of the Constituent Assembly and the Congress. A strong advocate of workers' rights and the rights of the rural poor, he was renowned for his courage, generosity and sense of fairness. He felt that the provinces of new India should be reorganized along linguistic lines—a demand the Congress had supported for years but done little to fulfil after 1947. Prakasam was among the leaders of a movement for a separate state for Telugu-speaking people. After several protests and some violent rioting, the central government relented, and a portion of the old Madras State was carved out to create Andhra state in 1953.

DOES INDIA HAVE A NATIONAL LANGUAGE?

Contrary to popular belief, India does not have one national language. The Constituent Assembly recognized a number of Indian languages and designated Hindi as an official language, along with English as a second official language until 1965. In 1967, the deadline for the use of English was extended.

SHANKARRAO DEO
1895–1974

Shankarrao Deo was a believer in Gandhi's ideas of non-violence, and an active member of the Congress and the Constituent Assembly, where he spoke eloquently on the issue of a 'national' language, arguing that India's diversity of languages and cultures must be respected. After Independence, he was a key member of the Samyukta Maharashtra Parishad, which sought a separate state for Marathi speakers with Bombay as its capital. But Bombay was a melting pot, and the large Gujarati community wanted the city to be the capital of their own state. It took years of protests, negotiations and violence for Maharashtra (with Bombay as its capital) to be finally created on 1 May 1960.

P Shilu Ao was a Naga political leader who played a significant role in the creation of Nagaland in 1963. Under the British, the various Naga tribes had retained a degree of control over their own region and affairs. With the coming of Indian independence, some Nagas sought to create an independent Naga nation, and engaged in a violent, bloody conflict with India. In the 1960s, more moderate Nagas like Dr Imkongliba Ao and P Shilu Ao chose instead to negotiate with the Indian government for a separate state for the Nagas within India. Ao was elected the newly created state's first chief minister.

P SHILU AO
1916–1988

LALDENGA
1927–1990

Like Nagaland, the Mizo Hills were part of the province of Assam at the time of Independence. However, the Mizos felt that the state government was insensitive to their needs (for instance, by not taking Mizos' fears of famine seriously). The Mizo National Front (MNF) was formed to fight for Mizo rights and political freedom. Under **Laldenga's** leadership, the MNF declared independence from India in 1966. This was followed by twenty years of armed struggle before a settlement was finally reached in 1986, which created the state of Mizoram on 20 February 1987 with Laldenga as its first chief minister.

4
FEMALE PIONEERS

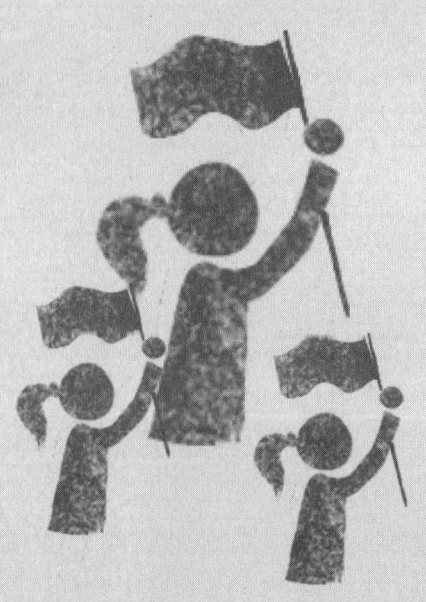

The government of India released a commemorative stamp on Kaur's birth centenary to honour India's first health minister.

A woman in power

Kaur was the only woman in the first cabinet of independent India and served as India's health minister for ten years. During this time, she helped set up several medical colleges and institutions, improved sanitary conditions across the country, oversaw programmes on maternal health and child welfare and worked towards reducing the spread of diseases like malaria and tuberculosis. Kaur was instrumental in founding the prestigious All India Institute of Medical Sciences (AIIMS), which continues to be one of India's premier medical institutions. She also worked closely with humanitarian organizations like the Indian Red Cross and St John's Ambulance Brigade. She received many honours for her dedication to improving public health.

Kaur represented India multiple times at the World Health Organization (WHO) and was the first woman and first Asian president of the World Health Assembly, the decision-making body of the WHO.

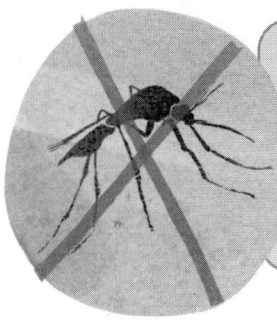

One of Kaur's most successful campaigns was waged against malaria, a disease that killed approximately a million Indians each year. Kaur successfully gained funds and material assistance from the United Nations to help combat the disease, and significantly reduced the number of people who died from it.

MUTHULAKSHMI REDDY
1886–1968

> "IT IS THE STATE AND STATE ALONE THAT CAN EFFECTIVELY BREAK DOWN THE TRADITIONAL CUSTOMS THAT ARE HARMFUL TO THE INDIVIDUAL AND TO SOCIETY."

An unusual family

Muthulakshmi Reddy was born into an unusual family: her father was the Brahmin principal of a college in Pudukottai (in present-day Tamil Nadu), while her mother was from the marginalized devadasi community. Reddy's father scandalized society by sending her to school, because girls, especially those with a devadasi background, were usually denied an education at the time. Reddy was academically gifted, and the Maharaja of Pudukottai intervened to allow her to study at the state-run all-male Maharaja College. Muthulakshmi would then go on to join the Madras Medical College, where she defied expectations by specializing in surgery, a field that few women chose. She later pursued advanced studies in England.

Set up in 1664 to treat sick soldiers employed by the East India Company, the Madras Medical College was only opened to Indians in 1842.

Devadasis were women who were 'dedicated' to temples as young girls, to be trained in the arts of music and dance, a centuries-old practice. They sometimes became courtesans who entertained kings and nobles. By the twentieth century, they were not considered respectable, and relegated to the fringes of society.

Fighting for women's rights

Alongside running a successful practice, Reddy argued for expanding women's rights. In 1926, she became the first female deputy president of the Legislative Council of Madras Presidency. She was also a member of the Women's Indian Association and wrote about and argued publicly on ensuring access to education, healthcare and voting rights for women. She was especially influential in helping to abolish the devadasi system. She also founded the Adyar Cancer Institute in Chennai.

AMMU SWAMINATHAN
1894–1978

"EQUAL RIGHTS IS A GREAT THING AND IT IS ONLY FITTING THAT IT HAS BEEN INCLUDED IN THE CONSTITUTION..."

The right to learn

Ammu Swaminathan was from Palakkad, in present-day Kerala. At the age of thirteen, she was married to a friend of her father's, Dr Subbarama Swaminathan, who was twenty years her senior. Young Ammu is believed to have only agreed to the marriage on the condition that she would be allowed to pursue an education after. Most girls who were married off young never had this chance, but Ammu was determined to make something of her life. In later years, she strongly advocated for a law against child marriage.

RUKHMABAI, THE CHILD BRIDE

Rukhmabai was married at the age of eleven. When she was older, she filed a case in court, arguing that she had never consented to the marriage, and that she would rather go to prison than live with her husband and give up her studies. The case was settled out of court. She went on to become one of India's first female doctors.

The good fight

Ammu, like many other educated women at the time, was swept up in the fight for freedom. She helped organize hartals, strikes and demonstrations in Madras (now Chennai) during the Quit India Movement. For her activities, she was arrested and sent to the Presidency Jail in Vellore. She was also a key member of the women's rights movement, and helped found the Women's Indian Association (WIA) in 1917, alongside Annie Besant and Muthulakshmi Reddy. She served a term as president of the Madras wing of the All India Women's Conference (AIWC). Both the AIWC and the WIA worked to combat the many discriminatory practices that Indian women and girls were subjected to. As a member of the Constituent Assembly, Ammu argued fiercely for the abolition of untouchability and for equal rights for women under Indian law.

TRAILBLAZERS IN EVERY FIELD

Despite facing social and financial challenges, many women in twentieth-century India fought hard to follow their dreams. Here are three women who were pioneers in their fields and role models for generations of Indian women.

ANNA CHANDY
1905–1996

Anna Chandy was born in the princely state of Travancore, in present-day Kerala. One of the first female postgraduates in the state, Chandy qualified as a lawyer and set up a criminal law practice. She later became the first Malayalee woman to serve, successively, as a first-grade munsif (a type of judge), a district court judge and a high court judge. Vocal about women's right to education and work, she was firmly against child marriage and purdah. For her views, Chandy frequently earned the disapproval of her male colleagues and peers. Undaunted, she founded a weekly women's magazine in Malayalam named *Shrimati* that was dedicated to educating women about their rights.

> "MY WISH IS THAT WOMEN SHOULD NOT BE WORSHIPPED LIKE GODDESSES. THEY MUST BE TREATED AS MERE MORTAL CREATURES... UNTIL THE DAY IN WHICH AN EVEN-HANDED STANDARD IS FORGED TO ASSESS BOTH [MEN AND WOMEN] THIS SORT OF GODDESS-WORSHIP REMAINS HOLLOW AND INANE."

THE MAHARANI OF TRAVANCORE

Anna Chandy was able to study law in the 1920s thanks to the forward-thinking queen of Travancore, Maharani Sethu Lakshmi Bayi, who championed women's education and promoted capable women to positions of power. Her aid enabled hundreds of women to study law, medicine, history, the natural sciences and mathematics.

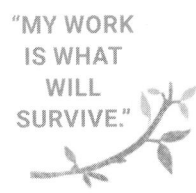

EDAVALETH KAKKAT JANAKI AMMAL
1897–1984

"MY WORK IS WHAT WILL SURVIVE."

Edavaleth Kakkat Janaki Ammal was born into a large backward caste family in Tellicherry (now Thalassery, Kerala). A nature enthusiast from her childhood, she was possibly the first Indian woman to receive a doctorate in botany in the US in 1931. Despite this, she was subjected to caste and gender discrimination back home in India. She moved to England in 1939–40 and did pioneering work on plant chromosomes and evolution. In 1951, now an internationally renowned scholar, she returned to India to take up a research position at Prime Minister Nehru's invitation. Among her many other contributions was the breeding of a new type of sweeter sugarcane that could be grown locally—this is still grown today!

SILENT VALLEY NATIONAL PARK

In the 1970s, the government wanted to destroy a tract of densely forested land to build a dam in a part of Kerala called the Silent Valley. However, environmental activists waged a successful, ten-year-long campaign against the dam, which threatened unique endangered species in the area. Ammal lent the weight of her expertise to show how important the valley's biodiversity was.

VIJAYA LAKSHMI PANDIT
1900–1990

Born Sarup Kumari Nehru, **Vijaya Lakshmi Pandit** was the daughter of Motilal Nehru and Swarup Rani, and the sister of Jawaharlal. Like the rest of her family, Pandit was committed to the independence movement and social reform. The first Indian woman to hold a cabinet portfolio in British India in 1937, she presided over the All India Women's Conference, was a member of the Constituent Assembly and headed India's first delegation to the United Nations. Known for being intelligent, frank, friendly and well-spoken, she was India's first female ambassador to several nations, and the first woman to be elected president of the United Nations General Assembly (in 1953). One of the most well-respected diplomats of her era, she helped create crucial international support for India during its first few years as an independent nation.

5
SOLDIERS AND SPYMASTERS

> "Professional knowledge and professional competence have to be acquired by hard work and by constant study. In this fast-moving technologically developing world, you can never acquire sufficient professional knowledge."
> Sam Manekshaw, 1998

When India gained independence in 1947, one of the most crucial things the new government became responsible for was defence. India would have to be able to defend itself from threats both from within the country and from outside its borders.

Fortunately, the British had left the nation with a well-developed armed force. The Indian Army had its roots in the East India Company's armed troops that safeguarded English trading centres and routes, while the Indian Navy's origins lay in the vessels that had protected the Company's trading ships. The Air Force had been founded in the early twentieth century and participated in World War II; it was small, but growing. However, all three had been shaped by British officers and British military practices. Similarly, India's main intelligence agency had been created in the nineteenth century to help the British stay ahead of their enemies.

Thus, the task for the government and for the few Indian military officers of high rank was to transform these colonial forces into national ones (or, as in the case of the Research and Analysis Wing, to build an entirely new agency) with new priorities and responsibilities alongside keeping the nation secure. The following pages feature some of the remarkable men who helped accomplish this.

KODANDERA SUBAYYA THIMAYYA
1906–1965

"A SOLDIER'S PROBLEMS TODAY STEM FROM THE FACT THAT, NOW, THE IRRESPONSIBLE USE OF MILITARY FORCE COULD DESTROY THE HUMAN RACE. A SOLDIER THEREFORE HAS A GREATER RESPONSIBILITY TO SOCIETY THAN HE EVER HAD BEFORE IN HISTORY."

Between two worlds

Kodandera Subayya Thimayya was born in Mercara (Madikeri) in the present-day state of Karnataka. He was among a select number of young men chosen to train at the Prince of Wales Royal Indian Military College in Dehradun, and then at the Royal Military College at Sandhurst in England. Thimayya (and others like him) occupied a complicated place in the colonial hierarchy. As a King's Commissioned Indian Officer, he was among the first Indians to be given authority over British troops, but even though he was the equal of a British officer, he continued to experience racial prejudice in social contexts. Thimayya was also sympathetic to the aims of the nationalist leaders but, as a British army officer in charge of keeping order, he frequently found himself on the other side of them.

> From 1917, ten spots were reserved for Indians at Sandhurst, the prestigious training institution for British army officers. However, very few made it through the selection process, which included tests and interviews with high-ranking army officers as well as the Viceroy.

A soldier and a strategist

When Britain deployed its colonial armies in World War II, Thimayya served with distinction, becoming the first Indian to command an infantry brigade on the battlefield in 1945. However, he is best remembered for his contribution

Thimayya and several other Indian officers considered resigning from the army to join the freedom movement. However, the Congress leader Motilal Nehru dissuaded them, suggesting that well-trained officers would be essential to the defence of independent India.

during the conflict of 1947–48. He first worked with the Punjab Boundary Force, helping to deal with the horrendous violence and the huge influx of refugees during Partition. Subsequently, he was given command of the Jammu and Kashmir force and joined the Indian army's operations in Kashmir. The former princely state had been invaded in October 1947 by tribal raiders from the newly created Pakistan. Thimayya's daring tactics helped the army successfully push the raiders back despite the punishing terrain and extreme cold. His successful exploits in Kashmir made him a household name.

One of Thimayya's best-known operations in Kashmir was an audacious tank assault on Zojila, a high mountain pass that linked Ladakh to Kashmir. It was the highest altitude at which tanks had ever been deployed, and they decisively tilted the balance in India's favour, and allowed Ladakh to remain protected.

Man of the world

Over the years, Thimayya gained the reputation of being an excellent soldier but also a man of great personal charm and diplomacy. He represented India internationally on several occasions, notably at the UN during attempts to settle the Kashmir conflict, and as chairman of the Neutral Nations Repatriation Commission in Korea in 1953. The latter was a complex job, and his efforts to be rigorously impartial brought him international acclaim. In 1964, Thimayya was asked to head the UN Peacekeeping Force in Cyprus. He died on duty at the age of fifty-nine.

In 1957, Thimayya was made Chief of the Army Staff. He was only fifty-one. Unfortunately, he and the defence minister at the time did not see eye to eye, which led to conflict. Things got so bad that Thimayya wanted to resign in 1959. But he agreed to serve his full term at the request of Prime Minister Nehru, and retired in 1961.

RAM DASS KATARI
1911–1983

Into the deep end

Vice Admiral Ram Dass Katari was a naval officer who served as the first Indian Chief of the Naval Staff. On the eve of World War II, Katari, like many other trained sailors, applied to join the Royal Indian Naval Volunteer Reserve. He served both at sea and on shore in several capacities, including sweeping for naval mines, transporting men and ships, and training men in anti-submarine manoeuvres. By the end of World War II, Katari was an experienced officer who had proved his worth. He was subsequently accepted into the Royal Indian Navy as a lieutenant commander.

Katari was among the first batch of young men trained on the Dufferin, a training ship (like the one shown here) set up in 1927 in response to Indian demands for maritime training opportunities. He did very well both academically and in the physical training activities and received the first Viceroy's Medal, which was awarded to the best cadet in a cohort.

From the old to the new

Katari held several important positions overseeing both the navy's personnel and fleet before he rose to the position of Chief of the Naval Staff in 1958. During these years, he helped lay the foundations of independent India's naval administration and management including the recruitment and training of Indian officers who could take up higher positions. As Navy Chief, Katari was constrained by a lack of resources and thus unable to expand the navy significantly. He focused instead on bolstering morale, promoting more equitable relations between officers and their men, and building India's indigenous capacities in defence production and maintenance as well as training.

When India became independent, there were very few senior Indian naval officers. Therefore, the government 'borrowed' British officers to fill senior posts up to 1958, when Katari took over from SH Carlill as Chief of the Naval Staff.

RD Katari had a passion for crosswords, which included both solving and creating them. He was the anonymous creator of *The Hindu*'s first cryptic crossword in 1971 and continued to create crosswords for the paper throughout the 1970s.

SUBROTO MUKERJEE
1911–1960

Taking wing

Subroto Mukerjee was a pioneer in the Indian Air Force and was India's first Chief of the Air Staff. He was born in Calcutta, into a large and progressive Bengali family. His father was a member of the Indian Civil Service, while his mother was an advocate of social change and a member of the All India Women's Conference. Educated both in India and in Britain, Mukerjee harboured an ambition to be a pilot and follow in the footsteps of his illustrious uncle, Indra Lal Roy, who had volunteered during World War I. Mukerjee got his chance in 1930, when the Royal Indian Air Force was set up. Mukerjee was one of the six cadets chosen via a competitive exam to be the first Indians to train at the Royal Air Force College Cranwell in England. In 1933, these men made history by becoming the first members of the Indian Air Force.

As Air Chief, one of Mukerjee's most vital tasks was modernizing the IAF's aircraft and equipment. One of the new planes acquired during his term was the Dassault Mystère IVA, the first transonic (very near the speed of sound) aircraft used in India.

Mukerjee served under three British chiefs, gaining valuable administrative experience that enabled him to take over in 1954 as the IAF's first Indian chief and shape the future of the Indian Air Force.

In full flight

As one of the IAF's earliest members, Mukerjee played a foundational role in how the IAF was administered and operated, as well as in how its members related to each other (for instance, he is believed to have helped introduce inter-community dining, where servicemen of all castes and religions ate together). In the late 1930s, Mukerjee and the IAF undertook their first real operation in the North-West Frontier Province, aiding the army's operations against the local tribal population. Here, Mukerjee earned himself a reputation for steadiness, quick thinking and compassion. Over the next few years, he grew to be the IAF's most senior officer, the first Indian to command a squadron and a station, and to be appointed Deputy Chief of Air Staff in 1947.

MEN ON A MISSION

India's new leaders knew well that newly independent nations could also be vulnerable. The men featured on these pages helped build India's defence capabilities, and ensured that the nation could respond strongly to threats.

KODANDERA MADAPPA CARIAPPA
1899–1993

> "NO ONE CAN BE A LEADER UNLESS HE SETS A PERSONAL EXAMPLE."

Born in Coorg (Kodagu), **KM Cariappa's** life involved several firsts. He was one of the first Indians to be inducted as a King's Commissioned Indian Officer, and the first Indian commander-in-chief of the army. He is credited with transforming the colonial army into a national army that was resolutely apolitical. He also did away with archaic British recruitment practices based on caste and regional biases, and established new units that recruited members from all castes and classes. Cariappa was known to be a stickler for rules, but also as an officer deeply invested in the well-being of his troops, ex-servicemen and their families. He continued to visit the troops to improve morale after he had retired, especially during the wars of 1965 and 1971.

In 1986, he was elevated to the rank of Field Marshal (the highest in the army). He was the second of only two army officers ever so honoured. The day Cariappa took over as Army Chief, 15 January, is now celebrated every year as Army Day.

SAM HORMUSJI FRAMJI JAMSHEDJI MANEKSHAW
1914-2008

SHFJ Manekshaw was a decorated military commander and the first Indian officer to be awarded the rank of Field Marshal. He was a charismatic leader known for his quick wit and direct manner, and was beloved by the men he commanded. Born into a Parsi family in Amritsar, he received his commission in 1934 and spent nearly forty years in the army. During this time, Manekshaw served in a variety of capacities but is best remembered for leading the Indian army during the war in East Pakistan (Bangladesh). Always plain-spoken, he opposed the Indian government's desire to go to war in April, suggesting that victory could be assured if the army had more time to prepare and avoided the monsoon. He was proven right when India defeated West Pakistan in December 1971.

As a young captain serving in Burma in World War II, Manekshaw was severely injured by machine-gun fire during a brave charge against the Japanese. He was not expected to survive, so a British major-general who was nearby pulled off his own Military Cross ribbon and pinned it on Manekshaw, saying, "A dead person cannot be awarded a Military Cross."

RAMESHWAR NATH KAO
1918-2002

"KNOWLEDGE IS POWER AND THE PROVERB HOLDS TRUE FOR INTELLIGENCE AGENCIES MORE THAN ANY OTHER ENTITY."

RN Kao was the founding director of the R&AW or RAW. He began his career in the police before moving to the Intelligence Bureau (IB), India's only intelligence agency at the time. In 1968, Prime Minister Indira Gandhi asked Kao to set up a new agency to gather information on external threats. As R&AW's first head, Kao had to set up the agency's capacities, create infrastructure and systems, and deploy covert agents—spies—in key locations across the world. Of special interest were India's neighbours, Pakistan and China. Information gathered by R&AW helped India to victory in 1971.

6
A DIFFERENT KIND OF POLITICS

> "...Democracy means that nobody has any perpetual authority to rule, but that rule is subject to sanction by the people and can be challenged in the House* itself. You will see how important it is to have an opposition. Opposition means the government is always on the anvil. The government must justify every act that it does to those of the people who do not belong to its party."
>
> BR Ambedkar, 1948

The Indian National Congress was the dominant political organization of the independence movement. During those turbulent years, the party came to include several factions or groups within it, with differing beliefs but united by the goal of a free nation. However, these factions and their charismatic leaders often had opposing ideas of what that free nation should look like and how to work towards it. They also differed on how India's government should be structured and what its responsibilities should be.

After 1947, several of these groups broke away and formed separate political parties. Over time, other parties that represented different social or religious groups or whose members were united by specific goals also came to exist. Often, the members of these parties were dissatisfied with or disagreed with the Congress on major issues. Therefore, even though the Congress dominated the political scene from 1947 to 1977, India's many other political parties played the role of the Opposition in Parliament.

A strong opposition plays an important role in the political life of a democracy. They critique the ruling government's policies, and ask questions to help keep it in check. They also offer a diversity of perspectives on key issues. In India's federal system, they have also ensured that states have a greater say in and greater freedom to make decisions on issues affecting them.

In this section, you will read about some of the founders and leaders of these other parties and the impact they had.

*House here means Parliament.

ELAMKULAM MANAKKAL SANKARAN NAMBOODIRIPAD
1909–1998

"INDIAN UNITY CANNOT AND SHOULD NOT BE AT THE EXPENSE OF ITS DIVERSITY."

Breaking with tradition

Elamkulam Manakkal Sankaran Namboodiripad, commonly known as 'EMS', was born in the present-day state of Kerala. Although initially tutored in Sanskrit and religious scriptures at home, EMS broke with tradition to pursue a formal, modern education. He also fought against the traditional caste and gender-based discrimination practised within the Namboodiri community, which was one of the most orthodox and privileged in the state. A member of the Congress party in his youth, he participated in the civil disobedience movement, for which he was sent to prison.

Like many young people at the time, EMS joined the Congress party, and found himself gravitating towards the socialist group within the Congress, which included people like Jayaprakash Narayan, Kamaladevi Chattopadhyay and Ram Manohar Lohia.

The turn to communism

EMS spent his time in jail reading about revolutions that had taken place across the world. He was especially interested in the works of Karl Marx, whose ideas had given rise to the political philosophies of socialism and communism. In 1934, he was among the founders of the Kerala wing of the Congress Socialist Party (CSP). The CSP helped workers organize themselves into unions to resist exploitation. It also supported the peasant community in their agitation against upper-caste landowners, who had historically denied them fair treatment. These experiences eventually led EMS and several other members of the CSP to join the Communist Party of India (CPI) in the late 1930s.

A global first

An incisive thinker and writer, EMS wrote extensively on how communism could be adapted to address Indian caste and class inequalities. In 1957, he led the CPI to victory in the Kerala assembly elections and became the state's first chief minister. The government he formed was one of the world's first democratically elected communist governments, and thus attracted global attention. One of the reasons the election of the CPI to power in 1957 was so remarkable is because, in the years preceding these polls, the communists had been unwilling to participate in parliamentary democracy. Many credit EMS with changing this and proving that the communists could come to power in a peaceful manner. Between 1957 and 1959, the government initiated several measures to address historical wrongs, including land reform, raising the minimum wage and protections against dismissal and eviction for poor workers and peasants. However, widespread agitation against new education policies led to the government being dismissed in 1959.

Karl Marx (1818–1883) was a German philosopher and journalist.

Communism is a political ideology whose aim is the overthrow of capitalism and the creation of a world where people can live and work as equals. It is based on the writings of Karl Marx and Friedrich Engels, which were especially influential in the twentieth century.

A man with a legacy

EMS would have a second shot at governing Kerala in 1967, as head of a coalition government. Although the coalition did not last long, he managed to implement some of the policies he had been unable to earlier. EMS remained a key political figure within the CPI, and later moved to the Communist Party of India (Marxist) when the CPI split in 1964 over differences of opinion. After his second term as chief minister ended, he remained a vocal member of the Opposition, and continued to write extensively and speak publicly until his death in 1998 (although he retired from active politics in 1991).

The two EMS-led governments are believed to have laid the foundations for Kerala's remarkable economic development. Poverty levels in Kerala are far below the national average, and the state has the highest levels of literacy and life expectancy.

CONJEEVARAM NATARAJAN ANNADURAI
1909–1969

"I SAY THAT I BELONG TO THE DRAVIDIAN STOCK AND THAT IS ONLY BECAUSE I CONSIDER THAT THE DRAVIDIANS HAVE GOT SOMETHING CONCRETE, SOMETHING DISTINCT, SOMETHING DIFFERENT TO OFFER TO THE NATION AT LARGE."

Finding a cause

Conjeevaram Natarajan Annadurai was born in the town of Kanchipuram in Madras State (present-day Tamil Nadu). Although their traditional caste occupation was weaving, Annadurai's family encouraged him to go to school, and to later pursue economics at Pachaiyappa's College in Madras. Annadurai became a voracious reader and a persuasive public speaker and writer. These talents and an interest in social reform led him to seek a career in public service. He found himself drawn to the Justice Party, which was active in local politics at the time.

> Brahmins (on account of their high caste status) were generally more privileged, had better access to education and thus got most of the better-paying jobs during the colonial period. The Justice Party, which saw the Congress as Brahmin-dominated, was founded to demand better jobs and educational opportunities for non-Brahmins.

Erode Venkatappa Ramasamy, better known as 'EVR' or 'Periyar', was Annadurai's political mentor. In 1925, he began the Self-Respect Movement to encourage rational thinking and the rejection of discriminatory social and religious customs. He was a fiery and provocative social reformer who attacked not only caste but also wealth and gender inequality.

Forging a new identity

Annadurai met Periyar in 1935 at a public political event; it was the beginning of a fruitful intellectual partnership. Dissatisfied with the Justice Party's narrow focus, the two men worked to transform it into a movement that would promote wider cultural and social change. They renamed the party Dravidar Kazhagam (DK). Alongside advocating women's rights and the abolition of

> One of the demands of the Dravidian movement was the creation of a separate nation called Dravida Nadu. The demand persisted well into the 1950s.

caste, they popularized the idea that south Indian non-Brahmins have their own distinct Dravidian ethnic identity. The DK focused on educating Dravidians (Tamils and other southern communities) about their rich history, language and culture, and demanded the rejection of Aryan (north Indian) cultural practices.

The imposition of Hindi has long been a hot-button issue in the south, especially in Tamil Nadu. The DK and its successor parties (the DMK and AIADMK), were opposed to making Hindi mandatory in schools as far back as 1937. Anna (as he was popularly known) was even imprisoned for his participation in the 1937 protests—it would not be the last time he was jailed over the issue.

Seeking political power

In 1949, Anna parted ways with Periyar over differences of opinion on both personal and ideological issues. Along with several other DK members, Anna then founded the Dravida Munnetra Kazhagam (DMK). The DMK harnessed the power of cinema, theatre and journalism as well as public conferences to take the party's message to the public. The party's membership grew at an astonishing rate through the 1950s, and it soon became one of India's strongest regional parties. In 1962, Anna was nominated to the Rajya Sabha, but his biggest moment came in 1967, when he took office as chief minister of Tamil Nadu. His tenure was brief, but his government's policies were aimed at social reform and inclusive growth—among the measures he introduced were free pre-university education for the poor, the legalization of self-respect marriages (conducted without priests) and increased reservations in jobs and education.

Among the younger DK members was Muthuvel Karunanidhi, a young scriptwriter. After Anna's death in 1969, Karunanidhi would take over the reins of the DMK, and eventually serve five terms as chief minister of Tamil Nadu. Actor MG Ramachandran was another of Anna's political associates who later founded his own rival Dravidian party, the All India Anna Dravida Munnetra Kazhagam in 1972. The two parties have dominated Tamil Nadu politics since 1967; although tainted by corruption, both embraced Anna's vision of a government focused on social justice.

A DIVERSITY OF VOICES

The individuals on these pages founded or led parties that offered alternatives to the Congress, and thus contributed to making India's political landscape more diverse.

SYAMA PRASAD MOOKERJEE
1901–1953

"THE JANA SANGH STANDS FOR CREATING CONDITIONS OF TRUE NATIONALISM IN INDIA WHICH MUST BE THE HOMELAND OF PEOPLE PURSUING DIVERSE FAITHS AND RELIGIONS...WE STAND FOR ONE COUNTRY, ONE NATION AND ONE CULTURE."

Syama Prasad Mookerjee was an educationist and politician from Bengal. An excellent orator and member of the Constituent Assembly, he was part of Nehru's first cabinet but resigned in 1950 over the government's policies on Pakistan. In 1951, he founded the Bharatiya Jana Sangh (BJS) to be the political face of the Hindu nationalist Rashtriya Swayamsevak Sangh (RSS). According to Mookerjee, one of his goals in founding the BJS was to establish a strong opposition in Parliament, as he believed this was an important part of any democracy. The BJS was the predecessor of the present-day Bharatiya Janata Party (BJP).

RAM MANOHAR LOHIA
1910–1967

Ram Manohar Lohia was a well-respected writer, activist and leader of the socialist movement in India. Believing that the Congress was run by an upper-caste, English-speaking political class, he was one of the founders of the Socialist Party, and argued that India needed to empower lower-caste and tribal communities. To achieve this, he suggested that a strong reservation policy (60 per cent reservation) be implemented in employment and education. Lohia is remembered for his fierce and uncompromising criticism of the Nehru government's policies, and for consistently putting social justice issues at the forefront of politics.

> "...EQUALITY IS PERHAPS AS HIGH AN AIM OF LIFE AS TRUTH OR BEAUTY..."

JYOTI BASU
1914–2010

Jyoti Basu was a politician who served as chief minister of Bengal from 1977 to 2000 and co-founded the Communist Party of India (Marxist). In 1977, the CPI(M) led the coalition of parties that formed the government in West Bengal. Under Basu's leadership, the government enacted land reforms that redistributed wealthy landowners' land to poor farmers, and created a strong village panchayat system for the state's rural poor. However, the three decades of communist rule in Bengal also saw economic stagnation and a high degree of corruption. Nonetheless, Basu is credited with bringing some stability to a state that had suffered a terrible famine in 1943–44 and violent communal riots during Partition.

> "WHEREVER COMMUNISTS CAN FUNCTION PROPERLY WITHIN A DEMOCRATIC SYSTEM, THEY WILL..."

KANSHI RAM
1934–2006

Kanshi Ram was a Dalit anti-caste activist and founder of the Bahujan Samaj Party (BSP). Born in Punjab, he believed that Dalits and other marginalized groups needed to fight for their rights and an egalitarian society. He encouraged Dalits to take pride in their origins, and argued that the marginalized could only truly create social change by wielding political power. To this end, he founded the BSP in 1984. Thanks to his efforts to build a support base, the party gradually gained ground and finally won its first parliamentary seats in 1989. Since then, the party has had a strong presence in the state of Uttar Pradesh.

> "I AM A RUSTIC MAN, AND LIKE A RUSTIC PERSON CHURNS CURD TO PRODUCE BUTTER, I, TOO, AM CHURNING SOCIETY."

7
INSTITUTION BUILDERS

Sukumar Sen (1898-1963), was a civil servant tasked with organizing India's first general election in 1952. He was the first Chief Election Commissioner, and set up many of the electoral processes and infrastructure India still relies on.

When India became an independent nation, the majority of its population was poor and illiterate. The government had to work hard and fast to set up organizations and institutions that would oversee key functions and kickstart development. Strong institutions, especially in education, science and technology, would be the foundations upon which a modern nation could be built. One of the biggest challenges that the leaders of new India faced was that many things had to be figured out from scratch, from how to conduct elections, to how to measure and use the country's resources, to how to ensure that all Indians had access to food, education and jobs.

Fortunately, scientists, industrialists, educationists and others who were experts in their fields came forward to take up positions of responsibility. Many of them came from relatively privileged backgrounds and had benefitted from being educated at premier institutions both in India and abroad. Fuelled by the desire to contribute to the country's progress, they helped expand India's capacities in fields like technology, agriculture and education, and encouraged economic development.

Among these individuals were the people profiled in this section. They laid the foundations of many of the institutions and programmes Indians continue to benefit from today.

ABUL KALAM MOHIUDDIN AHMED
1888–1958

"WE MUST NOT FOR A MOMENT FORGET THAT IT IS THE BIRTHRIGHT OF EVERY INDIVIDUAL TO RECEIVE AT LEAST BASIC EDUCATION, WITHOUT WHICH HE CANNOT DISCHARGE HIS DUTIES AS A CITIZEN."

A scholar and a fighter

Abul Kalam Azad, as he would come to be known, was born in Mecca, Saudi Arabia, to an Indian father and an Arabic mother. He grew up in Calcutta, where his father home-schooled him in a rigorous curriculum. This included the study of several languages as well as mathematics, philosophy, history and Islamic theology (Azad also taught himself English, despite his father's disapproval). As a young adult, Azad grew interested in the nationalist movement. Unlike some fellow Muslims, he became convinced early on that India needed to be independent of the British. He even founded a journal named *Al-Hilal* in which he argued for the cause of Indian independence, suggesting that Indian Muslims must work towards freedom. Azad was a talented and persuasive writer, and this repeatedly got him into trouble with the British Raj.

In the 1920s and 1930s, some Indian Muslims distrusted the Congress party and continued to support the British Empire. They were concerned that a Hindu-dominated Congress government would favour Hindus over others. The British stoked and exploited this fear as part of their policy to 'divide and rule'. Azad's courageous anti-colonial, pro-unity stance encouraged more Muslims to support the movement for freedom.

Azad the statesman

In 1920, Azad met Gandhi and became the first well-known Muslim in India to ally himself with the Congress. It was an important moment, for it represented the idea that Hindus and Muslims needed to work together to oppose the British. In the years that followed, Azad embraced non-violence and satyagraha, becoming one of the freedom movement's most visible and respected figures. He helped organize the party's election campaigns by raising funds and choosing candidates. He was also a prominent member of the Constituent Assembly and was outspoken about the importance of India being a secular nation.

Azad was appointed president of the Congress party in 1940. Both before and after 1940, he was arrested several times for his involvement in the nationalist movement.

Educating India

In post-Independence India, Azad had new challenges to face. As India's first education minister, he had a monumental job ahead: about 85 per cent of Indians were illiterate since education had historically been denied to the vast majority of women, the poor and those considered lower caste. Azad now set out to right these wrongs. His policy recommendations included free, universal and compulsory basic education for children, adult education programmes to address literacy gaps, scholarships and stipends for the underprivileged and comprehensive teacher training. Azad also oversaw the setting up of institutions to promote the study of traditional art, music and dance forms.

The first Indian Institute of Technology (IIT) was established in Kharagpur in 1951, during Azad's tenure. It was established as an institute of higher education that would not only offer excellent education on par with the best international universities, but also be a centre for research.

MONKOMBU SAMBASIVAN SWAMINATHAN
1925–present

"THE ELIMINATION OF HUNGER AND ITS REAL CAUSE, POVERTY, SHOULD BE AT THE TOP OF THE HUMAN AGENDA FOR COMMON ACTION."

Distinguished origins

Born in Kumbakonam in present-day Tamil Nadu, Monkombu Sambasivan Swaminathan is the son of MK Sambasivan and Parvathi Thangammal. The family was involved in the independence movement, and occasionally played host to Congress leaders, including Gandhi. While Swaminathan's father had made a name for himself as an excellent and compassionate surgeon, the extended family were agriculturists. Young Swaminathan thus spent his school holidays on his family's farms in Kerala, which sparked a lasting interest in farming methods and technology.

An event that deeply impacted Swaminathan was the Bengal Famine of 1943. The colonial government failed to address a severe shortage of grain thanks to its preoccupation with World War II. As a result, millions of people died of starvation. Swaminathan believed self-sufficiency in food production could prevent future famines.

The science of growing food

Swaminathan went on to study agriculture, plant genetics and plant breeding, both in India and abroad. During this time, the Indian government had begun to take steps towards improving the country's food security. The measures employed included changing who owned the land and how they held it (land reforms), increasing investment in agriculture and setting up dams and irrigation systems. The government also invested in studying scientific methods to increase agricultural yields. Upon Swaminathan's return to India in 1954, he engaged in research on two of India's staple crops, rice and wheat, and returned to his alma mater, the Indian Agricultural Research Institute in New Delhi.

Feeding the world

India's population had grown steadily since Independence, but the amount of food produced did not grow at the same pace. While in the US, Swaminathan had come into contact with a scientist named Norman Borlaug (who would go on to win the Nobel Peace Prize in 1970 for his work). Borlaug had developed a high-yielding and hardy dwarf variety of wheat that had been successfully grown in Mexico. Swaminathan invited Borlaug to come to India to see if this success could be replicated here. Following a fruitful visit and a successful test run, these seeds began to be distributed to farmers.

> **FOOD SECURITY**
>
> When India became independent in 1947, food security (simply put, having enough nutritious food available) was an area of concern. Despite having a large rural population engaged in agriculture, India did not produce enough food grain to sustain its population and had to rely on agreements with other nations to import enough food all the way up to the 1960s.

A green revolution

Swaminathan arranged for demonstrations of the new wheat in Indian farmers' own fields as a means of convincing them to grow it. He also helped modify the colour of the Mexican wheat from its original red to a more familiar amber, which made farmers more open to eating it. The efforts he made to work directly with farmers were crucial to the project's success. In 1968, India's wheat production grew from 12 million tonnes to 17 million tonnes, sparking what would be called the 'green revolution'. Since then, India's foodgrain production has risen consistently. Swaminathan's own career has also been distinguished: he has held numerous prestigious posts, both in India (notably in the Ministry of Agriculture and the Planning Commission) and elsewhere, and he was awarded the very first World Food Prize in 1987.

In 1968, the Indira Gandhi-led government issued this stamp to commemorate India's strides in wheat production. The success of India's green revolution spread to other countries as well, with several nations in Asia beginning to grow high-yielding hybrid varieties of crops.

VIKRAM SARABHAI
1919–1971

Sheltered beginnings

Vikram Sarabhai was the son of Ambalal and Sarla Devi Sarabhai, members of a wealthy industrialist family in Ahmedabad, Gujarat. His parents were very involved in their children's education, and set up a school exclusively for them with a unique curriculum. While his mother, aunts and sisters were active participants in the freedom movement, Sarabhai remained focused on academic pursuits. He was interested in science from an early age, and believed his most significant contribution to India would come from developing expertise in scientific study and research. He moved to Cambridge to study but was forced to return to India to continue his research when World War II broke out. He would return to Cambridge later to complete a doctoral degree.

> "A PERSON WHO HAS IMBIBED THE WAYS OF SCIENCE INJECTS INTO A SITUATION A NEW WAY OF LOOKING AT IT..."

Man of many talents

Sarabhai was primarily a scientist, but his wide-ranging education meant that he was a man of diverse interests. He wanted to use his wealth to set up institutions for scientific research and study. He encouraged international collaboration and knowledge-sharing between scholars. The list of institutions he helped establish is long: the Physical Research Laboratory, the Ahmedabad Management Association (which later became the Indian Institute of Management, Ahmedabad), the Operations Research Group (India's first market research agency) and the National Institute of Design are just a few of them! He also took over the management of his family's businesses, and expanded into new areas during his lifetime.

THE SCIENTIST AND THE DANCER

While in Bangalore in his early twenties, Sarabhai fell in love with and married the Bharatanatyam dancer Mrinalini Swaminathan. Mrinalini was the daughter of Ammu Swaminathan and the sister of Lakshmi Sahgal, both of whom also appear in this book.

APJ Abdul Kalam was one of the first recruits to join the emerging space programme under Vikram Sarabhai. He eventually went on to become the head of India's missile development programme, and later served as India's 11th president.

To space and beyond

Sarabhai is best known for spearheading India's space programme. He believed that satellites offered enormous opportunities for scientific research, and could be used to beam education into remote, inaccessible regions. It was a way to harness cutting-edge science for social change, something Sarabhai strongly supported. In order to help India set up its own space programme, Sarabhai worked with various government departments as well as NASA and other international agencies to secure both technological expertise and funding. He oversaw the launch of India's first rocket on 21 November 1963, and was instrumental in setting up the Indian Space Research Organisation (ISRO) in 1969. Since then, ISRO has made great progress, from launching India's first satellite (named Aryabhata) in 1975 to executing the Mars Orbiter Mission, India's first interplanetary mission, in 2013.

In 1974, a crater on the moon was named the Sarabhai crater in honour of Vikram. In 2019, India launched Chandrayaan-II, a lunar exploration mission, which carried a lander called Vikram.

MAKERS OF MODERN INDIA

The government of free India recognized that a strong nation could only be built on strong foundations. The individuals on these pages worked in a variety of fields to promote the nation's growth, and in time, help it to thrive.

HOMI J BHABHA
1909–1966

"PHYSICS IS MY LINE. I KNOW I SHALL DO GREAT THINGS HERE."

Homi Bhabha was a nuclear physicist who helped establish India's nuclear energy programme. He came to believe that India needed nuclear energy to develop its industries and cities, and his efforts resulted in the establishment of research institutions like the Tata Institute of Fundamental Research in 1945 and the Indian Atomic Energy Commission in 1948. The Department of Atomic Energy was created in 1954, and Bhabha was appointed its secretary. By 1956, India had its first nuclear reactor (which also happened to be Asia's first). A visionary scientist, Bhabha also held a number of high-profile appointments, including, notably, president of the United Nations Conference on the Peaceful Uses of Atomic Energy in 1955.

> The Atomic Energy Establishment, India's premier research centre for nuclear energy, was renamed Bhabha Atomic Research Centre after Bhabha's death. Prime Minister Indira Gandhi said at the time that his loss was a 'terrible blow for [the] nation'.

PRASANTA CHANDRA MAHALANOBIS
1893–1972

Prasanta Chandra Mahalanobis was born in Calcutta. An academically brilliant student, he studied physics and mathematics at Cambridge but developed an abiding interest in statistics. In 1931, keen to develop knowledge in this new field in India, he founded the Indian Statistical Institute. Mahalanobis would devise new ways of studying large amounts of data, and go on to use statistical methods to study India's resources and economy. A key member of the Planning Commission, Mahalanobis's statistical analyses were used to plan India's economy, as well as conduct large-scale surveys to assess the country's production capabilities. He also established the National Sample Survey to collect social and economic data over time. This survey continues to be conducted today.

VERGHESE KURIEN
1921–2012

Born in Kerala to wealthy Syrian Christian parents, **Verghese Kurien** qualified as an engineer in India before winning a government scholarship to study in the US. When he returned in 1949, he was sent to work at a government creamery in Anand, Gujarat. Anand had a cooperative of milk producers who had tried to cut out middlemen in order to sell their milk directly to buyers. Kurien began working closely with the cooperative, and helped use modern technology to process and store dairy products as well as market them effectively. The approach was spectacularly successful: from its initial capacity of 250 litres of milk a day, the cooperative in 2000 handled a million litres. Renamed Amul, it is one of India's largest food producers today. Kurien was subsequently appointed the head of a new National Dairy Development Board. In this role, he started a programme called Operation Flood, which was intended to replicate the Anand model across India. Thanks to Kurien's efforts and those of the millions involved in dairy farming, India is today the largest milk producer in the world.

8
TITANS OF INDUSTRY

Dadabhai Naoroji (1825–1917), a founding member of the Indian National Congress and the first Asian to be part of the British Parliament, was a businessman. He articulated the 'drain theory', which suggested that being part of the British empire was bad for India's economy, as wealth from the country was being siphoned off to Britain.

Some of the best-known Indian companies in the world today—Tata, Bajaj, Godrej, Birla—were founded in colonial India. However, the government's policies favoured European businesses, while Indians were restricted to operating in a few sectors. Indian industrialists had to cooperate with the British Indian government in order to ensure that their businesses could operate.

But in the late nineteenth and early twentieth centuries, Indian business leaders grew increasingly unhappy over the government's bias against them. Many among India's business class now began to lend financial and personal support to the Congress party and especially to Gandhi. It also seemed like sound business sense to cultivate relationships with the people who would in future form the government of India.

Nonetheless, many of these titans of industry appear to have been genuinely motivated by a desire to help India prosper, both economically and socially.

Many engaged in philanthropic activities, often in major ways. For instance, they donated large sums of money to causes they believed in, from women's education to famine relief. They also helped set up pioneering educational and research institutions. Some even took to local politics to improve sanitation and urban conditions. This section features some of the many Indian industrialists who, in different ways, helped make modern India.

GHANSHYAM DAS BIRLA
1894–1983

"IT HAS BEEN THE POLICY OF THE HOUSE OF BIRLA... TO HARNESS THE UNDEVELOPED RESOURCES OF THE COUNTRY, PROMOTE KNOW-HOW, CREATE SKILLED LABOUR AND MANAGERIAL TALENT, SPREAD EDUCATION..."

Challenging an unequal world

GD Birla was born into a Marwari trading family in Pilani, Rajasthan. Although he had little formal education (and was inducted into the family business from the age of thirteen), he was a voracious reader who read widely on everything from philosophy to geography to science. This helped him better understand the world around him and enabled him to engage with people from a variety of social backgrounds. Hard-working and intelligent, Birla was undaunted by the colonial government's biased policies. He managed to successfully break into the European-dominated jute industry in Bengal, and expanded the family's business interests into several new areas.

> Along with resistance from the government, Birla also faced opposition from the Europeans who owned most of the jute mills in India. His biggest competitor bought up all the land that he intended to buy. Birla also faced difficulty in securing a loan, and when he finally got one, it was at a higher rate of interest than that levied on British firms.

Birla was known for being careful, meticulous and thorough. He made it a point to be knowledgeable about the work he was doing. For instance, when he ventured into cotton manufacturing, he took the time to educate himself on every aspect of the process, including the most menial tasks.

A mediator and a pragmatist

Like his contemporary Jamnalal Bajaj (also featured in this section), Birla donated generously to the Congress and to Gandhi, with whom he had a close relationship. Interestingly, Birla was sceptical about the effectiveness of civil disobedience; cooperation and partnership were a better way forward in his view. As such, he performed the crucial role of being an 'unofficial emissary and honest interpreter' between Gandhi and the British from the 1930s. When the British began to grant Indians greater representation in government, Birla was instrumental in pushing the Congress to participate in elections and form provincial legislatures. He was also a frequent traveller between England and India, and met with British politicians and government officials to negotiate political measures that would satisfy both nationalist Indians and the colonial government. The reams of letters and documents that he wrote and that he is mentioned in testify to the central role he played in the movement.

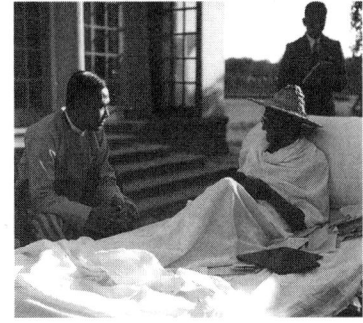

Birla helped to negotiate the Poona Pact in 1932. Earlier that year, the British had offered separate electorates to Dalits, a move Ambedkar supported and Gandhi opposed. Gandhi began a fast unto death in protest, but Ambedkar refused to back down. The Poona Pact, which guaranteed reserved seats for Dalits, was the compromise that was reached. In later years, Ambedkar vehemently criticized the entire episode.

Builder of institutions

Birla understood that economic and social progress were as important to India as political freedom. He therefore spent much of his wealth on causes he believed in, especially education. In 1929, he set up the Birla Education Trust, which oversaw the establishment of several educational, scientific and research institutions in his birthplace Pilani. He also supported eminent Indians in the arts and sciences, including Rabindranath Tagore and CV Raman, and helped fund both Aligarh Muslim University and Banaras Hindu University. He was a key member of and fundraiser for the Harijan Sevak Sangh, an organization founded by Gandhi in 1932 to work for the upliftment of 'untouchables'. Birla's philanthropy continued in the decades after Independence, with donations being made to hospitals, temples, museums and even towards the building of the first planetarium in the country in Calcutta.

Today, Birla's birthplace of Pilani is best known as the location of the prestigious Birla Institute of Technology and Science. Founded in 1964, it is still one of India's premier educational institutions and is known for its emphasis on practical training and holistic education.

JEHANGIR RATANJI DADABHOY TATA
1904–1993

"I DO NOT CONSIDER MYSELF TO BE AN 'ILLUSTRIOUS PERSONALITY' BUT ONLY AN ORDINARY BUSINESSMAN AND CITIZEN WHO HAS TRIED TO MAKE THE BEST OF HIS OPPORTUNITIES TO ADVANCE THE CAUSE OF INDIA'S INDUSTRIAL AND ECONOMIC DEVELOPMENT."

Scion of a noble house

JRD Tata was the son of RD Tata (a cousin of the visionary Jamsetji Tata, and a partner in the business) and his French wife, Suzanne. Young Jehangir's childhood was spent in India, France and Japan. He spoke fluent French and held both British-Indian and French citizenship until he gave the latter up. As a young man, his plan to study engineering at Cambridge was derailed by the outbreak of World War I. He undertook a stint in the French army, but did not resume his studies at the end of the war. Instead, he joined the family business as an unpaid apprentice in 1925, bypassing a university education altogether (something he regretted in his later years). When RD Tata died suddenly in 1926, Jehangir was left to take his father's place as director of Tata Sons, and shoulder the responsibility of caring for his family.

JAMSETJI TATA'S LEGACY

The Tata Group was founded by Jamsetji Nusserwanji Tata (1839–1901), who is often called the 'father of Indian industry'. Although he began as a cotton manufacturer and trader, the company he set up would go on to become one of India's largest industrial enterprises. JN Tata pioneered many progressive employee welfare schemes, including pensions and accident compensation. Among a variety of philanthropic donations, he helped fund the Indian Institute of Science, Bangalore, and endowed a scholarship that continues to help Indian students pursue higher education abroad.

In recognition of his efforts in laying the foundations of Indian industry, Jamsetji Tata's obituary said: "He sought no honour and he claimed no privilege; but the advancement of India and her myriad peoples, was with him an abiding passion."

Taking India to the skies

In 1938, JRD Tata was appointed Chairman of the Tata Group, which then consisted of fourteen companies in a variety of industries. His tenure, the longest of any chairman, would see the conglomerate grow enormously in size, and diversify into new areas such as chemicals, tea production and, most importantly, aviation. Tata had been interested in flying from a very young age, and was among the first Indians to earn a commercial pilot's license. In 1932, he started an airmail service, which became the foundation of India's first ever domestic airline, Tata Airlines. Renamed Air India in 1946, the airline was nationalized in 1953, and continues to be India's national carrier today. In 2021, the Indian government sold Air India back to the Tata Group.

JRD Tata helped establish the Tata Institute of Fundamental Research (which was instrumental in helping India's atomic energy programme get off the ground), the Tata Memorial Hospital (one of India's premier cancer research and treatment centres), the Tata Institute of Social Sciences and the National Centre for the Performing Arts in Mumbai.

Business with a conscience

While Tata was acquainted with several Congress leaders, and sympathetic to the freedom movement, he did not actively participate in politics. However, he was keen to contribute to India's growth and economic development in a significant way. In 1944, Tata and several other leading businessmen like GD Birla, Purushotamdas Thakurdas and Kasturbhai Lalbhai, formulated the Bombay Plan for developing the Indian economy. This revolutionary plan envisioned the government and industrialists working together to invest in and grow India's heavy industry—power, mining, railways, roads and iron and steel. The plan also dedicated large sums of money towards educational and social reform programmes. Although it was never implemented, it remains an interesting example of how early Indian business leaders viewed their role in nation-building.

JN Tata built India's first luxury hotel, the Taj Mahal Palace Hotel in Mumbai. JRD Tata helped make it successful and profitable.

EXCELLENCE IN EVERY SPHERE

Whether it was by directly participating in the nationalist movement, contributing money and expertise or building socially responsible businesses, the industrialists featured on these pages all found ways to participate in the important task of building a nation.

JAMNALAL BAJAJ
1889–1942

"JAMNALALJI WAS RATHER UNIQUE IN HIS OWN WAY...HIS ABSOLUTE INTEGRITY AND HONESTY OF PURPOSE ENDEARED HIM TO US."

Jawaharlal Nehru, 1951

Born into poverty in the princely state of Jaipur, **Jamnalal Bajaj** was the adopted grandson of Bacchraj Bajaj, head of a wealthy business family in Wardha, Gujarat. Jamnalal successfully expanded the business into what is today the Bajaj Group. Despite his wealth, he lived austerely, taking to heart Gandhi's philosophy that the wealthy are merely trustees who have a duty to use their wealth for social good. Bajaj saw Gandhi as a spiritual father, and the two men worked closely on Gandhi's constructive programmes in rural India. He served as the Congress party's treasurer for twenty years, and was involved in all of the party's major campaigns. Bajaj served time in prison for being part of the nationalist movement.

Jamnalal was married off at the age of twelve to the eight-year-old Jankidevi, who grew up to become a Gandhian in her own right. She spoke out against purdah and untouchability, and worked with other Gandhians in the campaigns they undertook after Independence. She was awarded a Padma Vibhushan in 1956 for her work.

Ambalal Sarabhai was born into a wealthy Gujarati merchant family based in Ahmedabad. He was one of Gandhi's earliest and most ardent supporters. Besides making large financial contributions, the Sarabhais were enthusiastic participants in India's nationalist movement. Their home in Ahmedabad was a meeting place for India's nationalist and intellectual elite, including the Nehrus, Vallabhbhai Patel and Rabindranath Tagore. Sarabhai was also a member of the National Planning Committee, an early version of the Planning Commission, where he argued for the importance of focusing on rural development. Sarabhai's children too played major roles in modern India. They included Vikram Sarabhai, the eminent scientist, and Mridula Sarabhai, the activist for social change.

AMBALAL SARABHAI
1890–1967

In his autobiography, Gandhi records the incident that led to his long association with Sarabhai. Gandhi had started an ashram on the outskirts of Ahmedabad but donations had dried up because people didn't approve of 'untouchables' being accepted into the ashram. Just when all seemed lost, Sarabhai arrived and made a donation of 13,000 rupees (a substantial amount at the time), thus saving the ashram from closure.

KHWAJA ABDUL HAMIED
1898–1972

A pioneering chemist and freedom fighter, **Dr Khwaja Abdul Hamied** was born in Aligarh. After some years spent studying in Germany, he returned to India and founded the Chemical, Industrial and Pharmaceutical Laboratories (CIPLA) in 1935. At the time, India was heavily dependent on foreign manufacturers for drugs. Hamied hoped, through the research and development of drugs, to help India become self-sufficient. He was also part of the Bombay Legislative Council and later appointed the sheriff of Bombay. Currently run by his son Yusuf, CIPLA manufactures high quality, affordable drugs, which have helped save lives all over the world.

"IT IS NOT BRITAIN ALONE WHICH IS RULING OVER US, BUT THE INTELLECTUAL AND INDUSTRIAL SUPERIORITY OF THE WEST."

9
LEADERS OF THE NATION

> "There comes a time in the life of every nation when it stands at the crossroads of history and must choose which way to go. But for us there need be no difficulty or hesitation, no looking to right or left. Our way is straight and clear—the building up of a socialist democracy at home with freedom and prosperity for all, and the maintenance of world peace and friendship with all nations."
>
> *Lal Bahadur Shastri, 1964*

The Indian prime minister is the head of the government and holds the most powerful political office in the country. Usually the head of the political party with the largest majority in Parliament, the prime minister has the power to set the priorities of the government and to choose ministers who will be closely involved in running the country. In addition to their governmental responsibilities, the prime minister is also the leader of the nation. In this capacity, they represent Indian democracy, and as such, are meant to be a unifying figure for India's many diverse communities.

Since 1947, fifteen individuals have held the demanding job of being prime minister. Some occupied the role for brief periods, interludes in which they were unable to have a long-lasting impact. Others remained in the role for years, and through their vision and leadership, shaped the nation in significant and enduring ways.

In this section, you will read about five people who have served as prime minister of India since 1947. Each of these individuals had markedly different beliefs about what India should be like politically and socially, what it means to be Indian and what the country's goals should be, both for its own people and as part of an international community. They also had widely divergent backgrounds, personal beliefs and political principles. That five such varied individuals have all held the highest political office in the land is indicative of India's political diversity.

JAWAHARLAL NEHRU
1889–1964

"...WHAT SHALL BE OUR ENDEAVOUR? TO BRING FREEDOM AND OPPORTUNITY TO THE COMMON MAN, TO THE PEASANTS AND WORKERS OF INDIA; TO FIGHT AND END POVERTY AND IGNORANCE AND DISEASE; TO BUILD UP A PROSPEROUS, DEMOCRATIC AND PROGRESSIVE NATION, AND TO CREATE SOCIAL, ECONOMIC AND POLITICAL INSTITUTIONS WHICH WILL ENSURE JUSTICE AND FULLNESS OF LIFE..."

Leading by example

Jawaharlal Nehru was born in Allahabad (present-day Prayagraj) to Motilal Nehru, a successful barrister, and his wife Swarup Rani. Young Jawaharlal's upbringing was more in keeping with British than Indian norms: he was first tutored at home, and then spent several years in England at Harrow (a prestigious boys' school), the University of Cambridge and in London. He returned to India in 1912. His father was one of the leaders of the Congress, and Nehru soon began to work alongside him in the nationalist movement. The family home in Allahabad became a centre of anti-colonial activity and Jawaharlal gained recognition and popularity as an intelligent, principled young leader who was able to mediate between factions with opposing ideologies. He was among the first to urge that Indians demand 'purna swaraj' (complete self-rule) and was instrumental in formulating the goal of a secular, democratic nation.

The British saw Nehru as a threat, because of which he spent almost nine years in prison. Often housed in poor conditions, he threw himself into reading and writing, and produced several books that remain popular today.

Making modern India

With the looming departure of the British in 1947, several issues confronted Nehru and the Congress leadership. The most pressing was how to create a united political entity out of hundreds of princely states and British-ruled provinces whose inhabitants had not much in common. Nehru's response was to envision a pluralistic India, where varied communities were united by a shared identity that went beyond caste, religious and other divisions. Another urgent concern was the crushing poverty and economic deprivation most Indians faced. Nehru's belief in socialism led him to emphasize the government's role in empowering people to rise out of poverty. These ideas of India came to underpin the principles of the Constitution as well as the government's policies after 1947.

The Cold War is the name of the period of global tension between the democratic United States of America and the communist Soviet Union (and their allies). This tension determined how countries related to each other, what wars they fought and whom they gave aid to. Rather than align with one or the other, Nehru believed India would be best served by remaining non-aligned and thus retain its independence.

An indelible legacy

Nehru remains India's longest-serving prime minister—he was in office for nearly eighteen years before his death. During that time, he often worked seventeen-hour days and made it a point to participate in parliamentary discussions and answer questions on his policies. He thus fostered a respect for and trust in the mechanisms of democracy. He also supported the founding of long-lasting institutions in the areas of science, technology and the arts. His belief in the need for infrastructure and heavy industry led to investment in these areas, including the construction of large dams and facilities that remain in operation today. Most importantly, he kept the fragile new country together through several crises, including communal violence, war, food shortages, agitation in the states and disagreements within the government. This, perhaps, is his most enduring legacy, an ideal for successive generations to strive towards: a democratic, modern, culturally diverse and yet united India.

Even after he took office, Nehru made it a point to make time to listen to ordinary Indians' concerns. Members of the public could visit the prime minister in his residence to bring matters to his attention. Today, the residence he occupied is a library and museum.

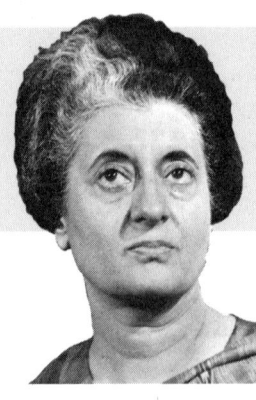

INDIRA PRIYADARSHINI GANDHI
1917–1984

"I DO NOT CARE WHETHER I LIVE OR DIE...I HAVE LIVED A LONG LIFE AND I AM PROUD THAT I SPENT THE WHOLE OF MY LIFE IN THE SERVICE OF MY PEOPLE."

The centre of politics

Indira Gandhi, India's only female prime minister, was the daughter of Jawaharlal and Kamala Nehru. After a childhood at the centre of politics, Indira joined the Congress at twenty-one. She was chosen to succeed Lal Bahadur Shastri as the leader of the party in 1966, when the latter died unexpectedly. The Congress Syndicate (a small, powerful group within the party) had chosen Indira as they believed she was inexperienced and could be easily controlled. She proved them all wrong by swiftly seizing power and splitting the party in two. In 1971, she further strengthened her position by leading her party to a large electoral victory.

Indira's grandparents, parents, aunts, uncles and cousins were all active in the nationalist movement and she too was drawn into it. At four, she sat on her grandfather's lap during his trial (Motilal Nehru was arrested by the British for organizing a hartal). At twelve, she helped found the Vanar Sena, a Congress children's group that was active in the 1930s. At university in England, she campaigned to gain public support for the movement.

Democracy and dissent

During her first full term as prime minister, Indira implemented populist measures that had faced opposition from her former party colleagues. She also altered the character of the central government, the bureaucracy and the judiciary by centralizing power in the hands of the prime minister and preferentially appointing her supporters (often friends and family members) to high positions. This inevitably led to corruption and nepotism, and rising prices and food shortages after successive failed monsoons created public discontent. The public's dissatisfaction manifested in a popular movement against the Congress in 1974. Led by Jayaprakash Narayan, the goal of the movement was the removal of Indira Gandhi and the corrupt Congress, and a 'total revolution' in Indian society and politics.

A state of emergency

On 26 June 1975, alleging that the country faced a threat to its unity, Indira declared a state of emergency. The Emergency lasted for twenty-one months, during which time Opposition leaders and activists were jailed, non-Congress state governments dismissed, foreign journalists sent out of the country and the press heavily censored. The Constitution was changed to give Parliament more power and to protect its actions from being challenged in court.

Two controversial campaigns, slum demolition in Delhi and a sterilization programme to enforce family planning, were implemented despite widespread resistance. The repressive Emergency was the greatest challenge Indian democracy had ever faced—and it ended only when Indira herself surprisingly called for fresh elections in 1977.

Indira and her Congress were defeated in the 1977 elections, and the Janata Party, which included many of Indira's opponents, formed the government. Indira's old rival Morarji Desai was appointed prime minister but his government did not last its full term.

India and Indira

Despite the Emergency, Indira Gandhi was voted back into power in 1980 on a wave of popular support, especially among poorer Indians. Today, she is remembered for her cult of personality and anti-democratic tendencies. However, she continues to command respect for her strong leadership during the 1971 war, and for her support for the Green Revolution, which allowed India to become self-reliant in food production. She also made contributions to India's conservation policies (including overseeing the launch of Project Tiger), approved India's first nuclear test explosion in Pokhran in 1972 (which made India officially a nuclear power) and oversaw the establishment of the Indian Space Research Organisation.

Indira was assassinated by her Sikh bodyguards in October 1984 in retaliation for the violent military action she authorized against Sikh separatists in the Golden Temple in Amritsar earlier that year.

LEADERS OF FREE INDIA

The three men on these pages, who had different backgrounds and divergent views on politics and economics, led modern India through some of the most eventful periods in its history.

MORARJI DESAI
1896–1995

"THE VERY SPIRIT OF INDIA ABHORS DICTATORSHIP."

Morarji Desai was a conservative Congress politician who was active in the nationalist movement and member of state- and national-level governments. In 1966, Desai hoped to become prime minister after LB Shastri's sudden death, but he lost out to Indira Gandhi. After briefly serving on her cabinet, he was, from 1969, one of her staunchest critics. His protests against her government led to him being imprisoned during the Emergency. He fought the 1977 elections as a member of the Janata Party and became India's first non-Congress prime minister. However, his tenure was marred by infighting among the parties of the coalition government and he resigned in 1979.

Hutatma Chowk [Martyrs' Square] in Mumbai is today a memorial to protesters from the Samyukta Maharashtra movement who died in police firing in 1956.
As chief minister of Bombay, Desai had given the order to fire. He was widely criticized for this.

PV Narasimha Rao, a scholarly Congress veteran from the Telangana region, was a key minister under Indira Gandhi and Rajiv Gandhi. In 1991, Rao became the first politician from the south to serve as prime minister. Almost immediately, he had to deal with a severe economic crisis. Despite leading a minority government, Rao and his finance minister Manmohan Singh implemented sweeping economic reforms. Their new policies encouraged private businesses to enter sectors previously dominated by the government, made it easier for Indians to start and run businesses, and encouraged foreign investment in India. This liberalization of the Indian economy kickstarted a period of economic growth and prosperity, although not all Indians benefitted equally from it.

PAMULAPARTI VENKATA NARASIMHA RAO
1921–2004

> "THE ONLY WAY TO EXIST IN INDIA IS TO COEXIST."

The illegal destruction of the Babri Masjid in Ayodhya by members of Hindu right-wing organizations occurred during Rao's tenure in December 1992. The incident triggered violent communal riots across India in which over 2000 people died and many more were injured.

ATAL BIHARI VAJPAYEE
1924–2018

Atal Bihari Vajpayee was India's first non-Congress prime minister to complete a full five-year term. A member of the Rashtriya Swayamsevak Sangh and Jana Sangh, Vajpayee was an excellent speaker and writer. He was first elected to Parliament in 1957. He would go on to be elected to the Lok Sabha several more times and spent a total of forty-seven years as an MP. In 1980, he helped form the Bharatiya Janata Party (BJP) and was its first president. He took office as India's prime minister in 1999, heading a coalition of twenty-four parties. During his tenure, Vajpayee made significant efforts to improve India-Pakistan relations and to end the violence in Kashmir. He also oversaw the further opening up of India's economy, which led to a period of steady growth.

> "OUR NATIONAL LIFE IS FULL OF VARIETY. THERE ARE MANY LANGUAGES, MANY SECTS, MANY MODES OF LIFE AND MANY STYLES OF ART AND LITERATURE. THIS VARIETY IS THE SYMBOL OF THE RICHNESS OF OUR LIFE."

10
GREEN WARRIORS

"The eradication of poverty in a country like India is simply not possible without the rational management of our environment..."
Environmentalist Anil Agarwal, 1985

After Independence, the Indian government emphasized the need for industrial development as a means of growing India's economy and lifting millions out of poverty. Inevitably, this put immense pressure on the natural environment, with widespread deforestation occurring as trees were cut down to make way for factories, mines, commercial farms and areas of land submerged by the construction of dams.

Although these projects were meant to help the poor, it has often been the case that the poor face the brunt of the consequences of environmental damage, such as floods, landslides and other natural disasters with man-made causes. India's wildlife, too, has come under threat, with many species of plants and animals growing ever more endangered in the years since 1947.

As a result, India has seen a number of popular movements aimed at protecting the natural environment from at least the 1970s onwards. There have also been numerous attempts at stopping the construction of dams that would displace large numbers of people (with little compensation for the loss of their homes and lands) and cause ecological damage to the surrounding areas. A rise in the environmental consciousness of the general public has also seen an increased emphasis on preserving the habitats of rare and endangered wildlife by designating certain regions as sanctuaries and national parks.

This section documents some of the Indians whose attempts to protect India's wildlife and natural environment have had significant impact on environmentalism in the country.

SALIM MOIZUDDIN ABDUL ALI
1896–1987

Finding a passion

Born into a well-off family in Bombay, Salim Ali and his siblings often went hunting when they were young, and shot down birds using their air rifles. When he was about ten, Ali bagged an unusual-looking sparrow with a yellow patch on its throat. Intrigued, he took the bird to the head of the Bombay Natural History Society (BNHS), WS Millard, to be identified. This was Ali's first encounter with the world of ornithology. It would spark a lifelong passion for observing and studying birds, which in turn led to Ali almost single-handedly transforming ornithology and conservation in India.

> The BNHS was founded in 1883 and remains one of India's largest scientific organizations focused on wildlife research and conservation. Ali served as an honorary secretary and was associated with the organization for most of his life.

From business to birds

Although Ali initially dropped out of college to manage his family's business interests in Burma, he later completed a degree in zoology. He was keen to make the study of birds in their environment his primary occupation and so sought training in Germany, under the well-respected ornithologist Erwin Stresemann. During his time here, he learned many new practices, such as bird ringing, which he would subsequently employ back in India. Ringing involves attaching a numbered ring to a bird's leg, which then allows the bird to be tracked and studied over its lifetime.

Between 1927 and 1929, Ali worked as a 'Guide Lecturer' in the Natural History section of the Prince of Wales Museum, Bombay, teaching schoolchildren and the general public about India's wildlife.

In the field

Upon his return to India, Ali realized that there were large areas of the subcontinent whose wildlife had not been documented or studied at all. He convinced the BNHS and rulers of several princely states in these areas to fund ornithological surveys. For the next twenty years, Ali travelled all over the subcontinent, from Hyderabad and Kerala to the North-East, observing, recording and collecting hundreds of species of Indian birds. These studies became the basis for several books that documented India's diverse avifauna, their behaviour and habits.

In 1941, Ali published *The Book of Indian Birds*, which was the first work of its kind in India and is credited with helping to popularize bird-watching and spreading awareness about the importance of conservation.

Looking to the future

Over the years, Ali grew into a well-respected pioneer of Indian ornithology. This enabled him to lend the weight of his experience and knowledge to conservation efforts. At different points, he helped convince Jawaharlal Nehru and Indira Gandhi, respectively, to protect the Bharatpur Bird Sanctuary (now Keoladeo National Park) in Rajasthan as well as the Silent Valley National Park in Kerala. For his work, he received several Indian and international honours, including the prestigious J Paul Getty Wildlife Conservation Prize in 1976, considered by some to be the Nobel Prize in the field of conservation. He donated most of the $50,000 prize money to the Bombay Natural History Society for the establishment of the Salim Ali Nature Conservation Fund.

GAURA DEVI
1925–1991

"WE HAVE NO QUARREL WITH ANYBODY BUT ONLY WANTED TO MAKE THE PEOPLE UNDERSTAND THAT OUR EXISTENCE IS TIED WITH THE FORESTS."

A woman of substance

Gaura Devi was born in a remote village in the Garhwal region of the Himalayas. Married at the age of twelve and widowed at the age of twenty-two, Devi had to work to support her young son. By the time she was in her fifties, Devi had grown into a well-respected figure in Reni and was even chosen to lead the local Mahila Mandal (women's group). During her lifetime, landslides and flooding increasingly came to impact people living in the region of Reni, and throughout the Himalayas. These landslides and floods were believed by the residents to be the result of years of deforestation.

> The communities that lived in the hills had traditionally relied on being able to access and use the forests for their livelihood. Their right to do so had first been challenged when the British introduced laws that brought the forests under the government's management. These essentially gave the government the right to fell trees for their own purposes and to sell off parts of the forests to commercial enterprises. These laws continued after Independence, despite the locals' demands that the government respect their traditional rights.

A fateful day

In 1973, a people's movement against the destruction of the forests began in the region. A fateful day brought Devi into the thick of it, when she led the women and girls of Reni into the forest to protect it from being cut down by loggers. Devi's courage in standing up to abuse and threats that day brought the 'chipko' movement into the limelight and encouraged women to join it in large numbers. The Chipko Movement has remained a landmark environmentalist movement for its adoption of non-violent methods and for its involvement of the rural poor, who are often the worst affected by environmental disasters.

KINKRI DEVI
1925–2007

"I HAVE TO DIE ONE DAY AND IT'S BETTER TO DIE FIGHTING FOR A CAUSE."

A difficult life

Kinkri Devi was born in Sirmaur district of Himachal Pradesh. Both poverty and caste prejudice prevented Devi from getting an education, and she began working while still a young child. She was married at fourteen but left home to fend for herself when her husband died of typhoid just a few years later. Despite her own troubles, Devi was deeply concerned about the environmental degradation being perpetrated in the Sirmaur region by mining companies. Their reckless and unsustainable quarrying had resulted in land and water pollution and the destruction of the region's natural beauty.

Limestone quarrying typically involves blasting the hillside apart using dynamite. In addition to destroying a part of the hills and causing pollution, blasting also weakens the rock and makes the area more prone to landslides.

Taking a stand

In 1987, Devi attended a seminar conducted by a local environmental group, which inspired her to take action. Now a frail fifty-five-year-old woman, she chose to take on forty-eight wealthy, powerful and politically connected mining companies. With the support of a volunteer group, she filed a Public Interest Litigation in the Himachal Pradesh High Court seeking a ban on mining in the area. When this failed to elicit a response, Devi began a hunger strike outside the court in protest. This helped focus attention on her case. Forced to look into the matter, the court finally ordered a stay on mining, later imposing a ban on blasting and directing the Ministry of Environment and Forests to undertake a study on the environmental impact of mining. The miners appealed to the Supreme Court against the decision in 1995, but they lost.

FIGHTING TO SAVE THE WORLD

The people in this section are notable for their willingness to take on the full might of powerful entities to help protect the natural world as well as vulnerable communities.

The people of the Bishnoi community of Rajasthan are often considered India's first environmentalists, as they follow a creed that requires them to protect and preserve the natural world they inhabit.

CHANDI PRASAD BHATT
1934–present

"I BELIEVE THAT ONLY A STRONG COMMITMENT ON THE PART OF THE PEOPLE CAN SAVE MOTHER EARTH."

Chandi Prasad Bhatt was born in the mountainous region of present-day Uttarakhand. Deeply influenced by Gandhi's call to serve, he dedicated himself from a young age to working for the welfare of people in his home district, Mandal. In 1973, Bhatt mobilized villagers in Mandal to resist the commercial felling of trees through non-violent methods. This was where the first instance of 'chipko' occurred, when Bhatt suggested that the villagers hug the trees to protect them. The protest was a success, and sparked a movement that spread across the region and remains an inspiration to environmentalists everywhere.

Sunderlal Bahuguna was also a native of Uttarakhand and a Gandhian like Bhatt. He participated in the freedom movement, and was involved in campaigns against untouchability and for women's education and the environment. In the 1970s, he became one of the Chipko movement's most visible and tireless leaders. He employed non-violent methods including demonstrations, marches and fasts in an attempt to spread awareness and prevent environmental destruction. A fast he went on in 1981 led to a fifteen-year ban on commercial logging in Uttarakhand.

SUNDERLAL BAHUGUNA
1927–2021

FATEH SINGH RATHORE
1938–2011

> "IF I DIE, I DIE, BUT WE MUST NOT LET THIS PLACE DIE… IT BELONGS TO US AND TO OUR CHILDREN AND GRANDCHILDREN."

Fateh Singh Rathore was an officer of the Indian Forest Service. In 1973, he was sent to Ranthambhore, a reserve under the Project Tiger programme. In order to protect the park's tiny tiger population and their habitat, Rathore resettled villages located in the park, and secured bans on activities that would disrupt the ecosystem. He was Field Director of Ranthambhore for ten years and later worked as an independent tiger conservationist, studying and reporting on the park's growing tiger population. Despite political apathy and even the threat of physical violence, he remained committed to his cause.

Medha Patkar is one of the primary organizers of the Narmada Bachao Andolan (NBA), a people's movement that opposes the construction of dams on the Narmada River. Beginning in 1985, Patkar has been at the forefront of non-violent protests against the Narmada Valley Development Project, which has already and will continue to negatively affect both people and the environment. The NBA's work on the human and ecological costs helped push the World Bank to withdraw funding from the project in 1993.

MEDHA PATKAR
1954–present

11
RECLAIMING ART AND CULTURE

> "Nothing is more advantageous than a rich heritage but nothing is more dangerous than to sit back and live on that heritage. A nation cannot prosper if it merely imitates its ancestors. What builds a nation is creative, inventive and vital activity."
>
> *Jawaharlal Nehru, 1950*

Many of the dance forms, musical styles and crafts that are studied, performed and produced across the subcontinent have existed for hundreds of years. After 1947, it was one of the priorities of the new nation to build institutions to encourage the preservation of these aspects of Indian culture, as well as to educate both Indians and those outside India about the rich and varied cultural heritage of the country. Accordingly, the first few decades after Independence saw the founding of several national institutions for the promotion of the arts, such as the national academies for music, dance, drama and literature. These were meant not just to preserve existing knowledge of ancient Indian art forms, but to encourage young people to learn and practise them. Some museums and the Archaeological Survey of India had already been set up by the British and now institutions were now set up and policies made to ensure the conservation of India's historical monuments and artefacts.

There were also many programmes aimed at reviving the traditional handicrafts industry, which had suffered during the British colonial period. Knowledge of the methods used was largely confined to the small communities that produced these items, and there was an urgent need to revive dying crafts and techniques and help support the people who engaged in making handloom and handicraft artefacts.

The individuals in this section are just a few of the many people who worked towards preserving India's centuries-old cultural and artistic heritage.

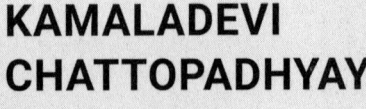

KAMALADEVI CHATTOPADHYAY
1903-1988

From tragedy to triumph

Kamaladevi Chattopadhyay was born to Ananthaya Dhareshwar and Girjabai in Mangalore (now Mengaluru). Although she grew up in a liberal, reformist atmosphere, young Kamaladevi had to weather several tragedies. Her father died unexpectedly, leaving the family in financial disarray, two of her sisters were trapped in abusive marriages and died young, and she herself lost her husband within a year of being married. These experiences brought home to her the importance of women's rights and a gender-just society. Meeting social reformers and political activists like Annie Besant, Pandita Ramabai, Gopal Krishna Gokhale and MK Gandhi also inspired her to involve herself in the freedom movement.

> "I WISH TO PROVE TO THE WORLD THAT A WOMAN CAN FIGHT AND FIGHT WELL IN SPITE OF EVERYTHING."

In England, Chattopadhyay pursued a diploma in social work, which took her to the slums and alleys of London's notorious East End. Here, she would mix with people from diverse social backgrounds and gain a good grounding in the practical aspects of social work.

While living in Madras, Kamaladevi came into contact with the vibrant Chattopadhyay family, whose members included the poet and Congress leader Sarojini Naidu, Communist party leader Suhasini Chattopadhyay and the poet Harindranath Chattopadhyay. She married Harindranath in a civil ceremony in 1919 and followed him to Cambridge; the marriage eventually ended in divorce.

Leading women forward

Chattopadhyay followed in the tradition of her mother and grandmother, both educated women who were unafraid to defy social convention. In the 1920s she was the first woman to contest in a legislative assembly election in India. She lost by a narrow margin. Soon after, she was appointed General Secretary of the All India Women's

Conference, the organization set up to expand educational opportunities for women. She also joined the Congress, and was among the first women to participate in the civil disobedience movement (and be arrested for it). She led from the front, and her example encouraged many more women across class lines to take to the streets and march for freedom.

When Gandhi first proposed the salt march to Dandi, he had not intended for women to participate. Along with Sarojini Naidu, Chattopadhyay convinced him otherwise. She herself was among a small group that marched to Chowpatty beach in Bombay and made salt there.

Looking to the future

After 1947, Chattopadhyay threw herself into several tasks, including the rehabilitation of Partition refugees. But arguably her most important contribution was her role in encouraging the production and preservation of Indian handicrafts and handloom goods. Many traditional crafts had been replaced by factory goods during colonial rule, with craftsmen suffering as a result. Appointed Chairman of the All India Handicrafts and Handloom Board, she enlisted talented professionals to create channels for the production, marketing and sale of handcrafted products. She travelled extensively to survey the state of these communities and their art, and oversaw the setting up of schools, institutions and design centres that would preserve and promote traditional techniques. Her interest in reviving traditional crafts extended beyond India; it was through her efforts that the World Crafts Council, an organization affiliated to UNESCO, came into being.

Among the crafts that Chattopadhyay helped preserve is the art of kalamkari, practised in the region of Andhra Pradesh. It involves the creation of block-printed textiles using vegetable dyes.

KAPILA VATSYAYAN
1928–2020

"...WE HAVE YET MANY MOUNTAINS TO SCALE AND RIVERS TO CROSS AND BOULDERS TO BREAK BEFORE THE VAST TREASURES OF THE INDIAN ARTS CAN BE FULLY EXCAVATED..."

Dancer, scholar, writer

Kapila Vatsyayan was born in British India into an unusual family. Reformist and liberal in their outlook, they were involved in the freedom movement and in the arts. Thus, Vatsyayan's own exposure to Indian art forms began early: she trained in a number of dance forms, including Kathak, Manipuri and Bharatanatyam, and studied English literature at university. She subsequently won a scholarship that took her to the US. It was here that she learned to combine her practical understanding of Indian art forms with theory and scholarship, and realized the importance of applying a serious academic approach to Indian art.

Vatsyayan was a founding member of the Indira Gandhi National Centre for the Arts and a life trustee of the India International Centre, New Delhi. While the former is under the Ministry of Culture, the latter is a non-governmental organization that serves as a meeting place for people involved in arts, culture, politics and public policy.

> Vatsyayan studied Kathak under Acchan Maharaj, father of the renowned kathak dancer Pandit Birju Maharaj.

A national treasure

Vatsyayan combined the skills of a well-respected researcher and scholar with those of an effective administrator. She was tireless in her attempts to bring Indian performers and artists to international notice, advocated the inclusion of arts education in schools and sought to shine a light on India's classical art forms as well as its many folk traditions. For instance, she played a key role in making the annual Republic Day parade a show of India's rich folk dances and music. She was also nominated to the Rajya Sabha, and advised three prime ministers—Jawaharlal Nehru, Indira Gandhi and Rajiv Gandhi—on the running of India's cultural institutions.

BAL KRISHEN THAPAR
1921–1995

Uncovering history

Bal Krishen Thapar was born in Ludhiana and studied history at university. Having developed an interest in the discipline of archaeology, he joined the Indian School of Field Archaeology in 1944, where he trained under the British archaeologist Sir Mortimer Wheeler. Wheeler had pioneered the use of scientific techniques in the field, which Thapar would continue to rely on these during his long stint at the Archaeological Survey of India (ASI). Meticulous and single-minded, Thapar participated in several important excavations, including at the Somnath temple in Gujarat, the Harappan site of Kalibangan in Rajasthan and in Afghanistan. In 1978, he was appointed Director-General of the ASI.

Preserving the past for the future

Over the years, Thapar gained a stellar reputation both at home and abroad. His work helped expand what was then known about ancient India, but his impact does not end there. He was a founder member of the Indian National Trust for Art and Cultural Heritage (INTACH) in 1984. INTACH is a non-governmental organization that undertakes the preservation of monuments that fall outside the ASI's purview. It works to spread awareness of the importance of heritage, and involves the general public in conserving monuments. It also collaborates with both government and international agencies to protect sites of historical and cultural significance.

Archaeology in India grew into a more serious undertaking in the late nineteenth century. The ASI was set up in 1861 to survey and document India's ancient monuments. It oversees archaeological research and the preservation of monuments across the country.

Sir Mortimer Wheeler headed the ASI from 1944 to 1948. He was involved in excavations of many important historical sites, where he employed methods that would make a lasting impact on the field. Sadly, his legacy is today tainted by evidence of harassment and racism while on assignment in India.

ARTISTS WHO TOUCHED NEW HEIGHTS

This section focuses on three remarkable people who, through their achievements and contributions, shone a spotlight on India's artistic traditions and influenced subsequent generations of artists and performers.

BISMILLAH KHAN
1916–2006

"MUSIC HAS NO CASTE."

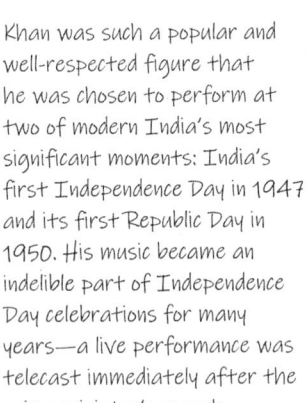

Bismillah Khan was born in Bihar, into a family of court musicians. Khan was taught to play the shehnai by his uncle Ali Baksh, a musician who played at the Vishwanath temple in Varanasi. Typically played only at religious ceremonial occasions or weddings, Khan elevated the shehnai to an instrument played simply for aesthetic pleasure, like the veena or the tabla. His inventiveness changed perceptions of how the shehnai could be played and the kind of music it could be made to produce. And, as a devout Muslim who performed frequently at Hindu ceremonies and temples, he epitomized India's syncretic history and religious pluralism.

Khan was such a popular and well-respected figure that he was chosen to perform at two of modern India's most significant moments: India's first Independence Day in 1947 and its first Republic Day in 1950. His music became an indelible part of Independence Day celebrations for many years—a live performance was telecast immediately after the prime minister's speech.

Jagdish Swaminathan was a journalist, critic and talented painter. In his work, he sought to break free of existing approaches to painting, arguing instead that art should more truly represent the world through the use of colours and shapes. He grew to be well-respected in the Indian art world, and helped establish Bharat Bhavan in Bhopal, an arts institution funded by the government of Madhya Pradesh. During his tenure as director of the institution's fine arts museum, he worked to bring tribal art and artists into the public eye, thus helping to promote and preserve some of India's oldest artistic styles.

JAGDISH SWAMINATHAN
1928–1994

Swaminathan 'discovered' the Gond artist Jangarh Singh Shyam, one of the first Adivasi artists to attain international fame. His distinctive style came to be called 'Jangarh Kalam', and his murals decorate parts of Bharat Bhavan and the Madhya Pradesh Legislative Assembly. Shyam's success helped many more Gond artists to take up painting as an occupation.

MADURAI SHANMUKHAVADIVU SUBBULAKSHMI
1916–2004

In 1966, Subbulakshmi was invited to perform at the United Nations in New York. This was just one of several international performances that established her as a cultural ambassador of India.

MS Subbulakshmi was born to a devadasi mother in Madurai. Trained to sing and play instruments from childhood, she began giving small public performances at just nine years old. Subbulakshmi moved to Madras at twenty, both to avoid marriage and to break free of the stigma surrounding devadasis. She proceeded to make a name for herself in Carnatic music, a historically upper-caste- and male-dominated field. Alongside mastering her craft, she also learned compositions from other Indian musical traditions and had a brief stint in film. Her efforts to capture a wider, pan-Indian audience elevated her to the status of a national icon. She was the first musician to receive a Bharat Ratna. She also received the Ramon Magsaysay award for her humanitarian and philanthropic activities.

12
LITERARY MARVELS

Literature flourished in many parts of British India but especially in Bengal. Rabindranath Tagore (1861-1941), India's only winner of the Nobel Prize in Literature, wrote in Bengali and translated his works into English.

From older works like the Vedas and the Tamil epics to medieval poetry, narratives and drama, literature flourished in the Indian subcontinent for thousands of years. However, a large number of Indians were denied education, which meant that access to written literature was limited. But, by the nineteenth century, more Indians had access to education (in English or otherwise), which also meant that more people were reading and writing about India.

With exposure to literature from Britain, Europe and the United States, Indians began to adopt new forms of writing to tell Indian stories. Short stories, poetry and novels in English and in major Indian languages became increasingly available to the reading public. Indians also began writing about their own history, social practices and religions, and articulating their political opinions in newspapers and journals. Writing was a good way to spread ideas. Everyone from social and religious reformers to nationalist leaders to poets, playwrights and novelists wrote about caste- and gender-based discrimination, colonial oppression and Indian history and culture.

Modern literature in India thus became a tool for social and political change, as well as a way for Indians—including the writers in this section—to explore (and sometimes rediscover) their identities, and the cultures and communities they belonged to.

MULK RAJ ANAND
1905–2004

"IF MUCH OF ENGLISH WRITING TODAY ESPECIALLY BY MEN APPEARS WITHOUT SUBSTANCE, IT IS MAINLY BECAUSE WRITERS LIVE IN BIG TOWNS AND HAVE LITTLE CONTACT WITH REALITIES OF LIFE ON THE LAND."

Man of the world

Born in Peshawar, Mulk Raj Anand was the son of Lala Chand Anand and Ishwar Kaur. Anand was educated in Amritsar before winning a scholarship that took him to England in 1925. Back home, Anand had taken part in the non-cooperation movement. Now in England, he worked with other nationalists to drum up support for Indian independence among the British public. In 1929, Anand completed a doctoral degree in philosophy, and subsequently worked as a lecturer. During his time in London, he was drawn to socialism and actively supported workers' strikes. His experiences convinced him that the poor all over the world faced similar struggles, which could only be alleviated through fighting for equal rights and the ending of discriminatory practices like casteism.

In 1927, Anand worked on the draft of his first novel, *Untouchable*, at Gandhi's ashram. Gandhi read the draft and advised Anand to simplify the language and make it seem more natural. He also advised Anand to travel through rural India and speak to people in order to understand them better.

Anand established connections with several well-known English literary figures, including EM Forster, who would later help Anand get his first novel published. Anand also wrote short reviews and articles for TS Eliot's literary magazine, *The Criterion*.

A writer and a radical

In 1935, along with other Indian writers and intellectuals, Anand helped found the Progressive Writers' Association. Among their goals was the promotion of a new literature that would address the many forms of prejudice and discrimination that prevailed in India. That same year, *Untouchable*, finally found a publisher after being rejected several times. It memorably depicts a day in the life of a young sweeper and highlights the hypocrisy and cruelty of casteism. In 1936, Anand published *Coolie*, a novel that focuses on the struggles of the working class. Themes of exploitation, poverty and social injustice continued to be central in all his literary works.

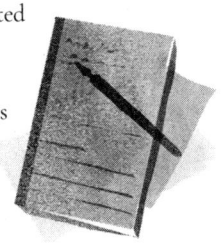

Blazing a trail

Anand returned to India after World War II and settled in Bombay. He wrote several more novels, many of them autobiographical. He was also a man of wide interests; both in London and back home in India, he wrote on a variety of subjects, from cookery to politics to folktales. Alongside writing, he taught at a number of universities, did charitable work and remained personally committed to fighting all forms of social and religious prejudice. Anand was among the first Indians to write novels in English that put caste and class struggle as well as the effects of British imperialism into focus. This helped make people both in India and outside the country aware of the terrible consequences of casteism and colonial oppression. Through his work, his politics and his articulation of what literature should seek to do, he left a lasting impact on modern Indian writing.

Anand attended the World Congress of Intellectuals in Defense of Peace, Wroclaw in 1948, where he met celebrated Spanish painter Pablo Picasso, Sri Lankan architect Minette DaSilva and American sculptor Jo Davidson, among others.

Anand, along with RK Narayan (also featured in this book) and Raja Rao, is considered one of the 'founding fathers' of the Indian novel in English. Narayan and Anand were notable for becoming widely popular both abroad and in India.

SAROJINI NAIDU
1879–1949

"AS LONG AS I HAVE LIFE, AS LONG AS BLOOD FLOWS THROUGH THIS ARM OF MINE, I SHALL NOT LEAVE THE CAUSE OF FREEDOM...I AM ONLY A WOMAN, ONLY A POET. BUT AS A WOMAN, I GIVE TO YOU THE WEAPONS OF FAITH AND COURAGE AND THE SHIELD OF FORTITUDE. AND AS A POET, I FLING OUT THE BANNER OF SONG AND SOUND, THE BUGLE CALL TO BATTLE."

A progressive family

Sarojini Naidu was the eldest child of Aghorenath Chattopadhyay, a scholar and educationist, and Varada Sundari. Born in Hyderabad, Sarojini grew up in a liberal, cosmopolitan and progressive household. The Chattopadhyays often entertained scholars, politicians, activists and artists, and encouraged their children to read widely and cultivate many interests. Sarojini and her brother Harindranath would go on to become well-respected poets, while her other siblings pursued careers in the arts and education or dedicated themselves to revolutionary and political activities.

In 1898, Sarojini Chattopadhyay married Govindarajulu Naidu, a young doctor she had fallen in love with some years earlier. Marrying outside of her caste was only one of the many unconventional choices Sarojini would make.

"Weavers, weaving solemn and still,
What do you weave in the moonlight chill? . . .
White as a feather and white as a cloud,
We weave a dead man's funeral shroud."

from 'Indian Weavers', which was published as part of Sarojini's first anthology of poems in 1905

The nightingale of India

Sarojini began writing poetry while still a child, but her early poems were deeply influenced by English literary traditions. While studying in England, she was advised by the poet and literary critic Edmund Gosse to refocus her poetry on India—the world she came from and belonged to. Sarojini subsequently turned away from her earlier imitative poems, and instead began composing poetry that reflected the sights and sounds of the subcontinent, and drew on Indian folktales and myths. *The Golden Threshold*, her first volume of poetry, was published in 1905, and received glowing reviews, both in India and abroad. She would go on to publish two more during her lifetime. She wrote in English, but the subjects she wrote about and the way she expressed herself remained distinctly Indian.

In 1930, soon after Gandhi was arrested for making salt on the beach at Dandi, Sarojini led a group of volunteers to raid the Dharasana Salt Works, as a way of protesting the unfair British law that prevented Indians from making their own salt. The protesters were met with violence by the police but did not retaliate. Sarojini herself was arrested and sent to jail; this was one of several jail terms she served during the nationalist movement.

A fearless trailblazer

From 1903–04, a time when Indian women were largely relegated to domestic roles and rarely seen in public, Sarojini began to involve herself in politics. Her ability to craft powerful speeches and speak fluently and persuasively made her stand out. She often spoke about the need for unity beyond caste and religion, as well as on the necessity of equal rights for women. She soon grew to be one of the most visible and well-respected members of the Congress (she was the first Indian woman to be elected the party's president in 1925), was a co-founder of the Women's Indian Association (WIA) and a member of the Constituent Assembly.

IDEAS OF INDIA

These three writers were born in colonial India, but their lives also spanned the struggle for freedom and the years after Independence. In strikingly different ways, each of them wrote stories that explore life in modern India in all its confusing, funny, sad and beautiful complexity.

RASIPURAM KRISHNASWAMI NARAYAN
1906–2001

"...IF A STORY IS IN TUNE COMPLETELY WITH THE TRUTH OF LIFE, TRUTH AS I PERCEIVE IT, THEN IT WILL AUTOMATICALLY BE SIGNIFICANT. BUT I NEVER THINK UP SPECIFIC PROBLEMS AND THEN WRITE A STORY ABOUT THEM. I WRITE THE STORY."

RK Narayan was born Rasipuram Krishnaswami Iyer Narayanaswami in the city of Madras. His first novel, Swami and Friends, was published in England in 1935 after several rejections. It remains a beloved classic even today. Like many of his later works, the novel is set in the fictional town of Malgudi in south India. Although these stories take place during the eventful pre- and post-Independence years, they are intensely focused on the personal lives of his characters. His stories are about people, their relationships and flaws, and the sorrows and joys of their lives, all told in his distinctive gently comic style. Narayan's work was popular both in India as well as abroad; among his many admirers were literary greats like Graham Greene, Somerset Maugham and EM Forster.

Malgudi Days, one of Narayan's short story collections, was adapted into a television series in 1986. Its title sequence includes sketches by RK Laxman, Narayan's younger brother, who was a celebrated cartoonist and the illustrator of his brother's books.

ISMAT CHUGHTAI
1915–1991

Ismat Chughtai was born into a large, liberal Muslim family in present-day Uttar Pradesh. She fought against convention to get a BA degree, train as a teacher and then work in Bombay. From the 1930s onwards, she regularly published short stories, novels and essays, and became a popular and pathbreaking writer of Urdu literature. Not only was she a woman writing about women's lives and desires (a subject not often dealt with in the existing literature by men) but she also adopted a direct, frank style full of the everyday language of the community she was writing about. Chughtai often attracted criticism for writing about taboo subjects that were considered 'unsuitable' for a woman to discuss, but, much like her characters, she refused to let social conventions dictate her choices.

> A major influence on Chughtai was Rashid Jahan, the outspoken Muslim woman doctor and writer. Jahan, along with three other writers, was part of the Progressive Writers' Movement in the 1930s. Their goal was to write literature that focused on people's lived realities, especially social issues that affected people's lives.

MAHASWETA DEVI
1926–2016

Born in present-day Bangladesh, **Mahasweta Devi** was a prolific writer and social activist. For much of her life, she travelled and worked among adivasis, Dalits and marginalized women. Their stories informed the many novels and short stories she wrote, which focused on caste and class struggle, gender discrimination and the violence of the state towards its own citizens. Through her writing, she highlighted the many forms of oppression faced by marginalized communities both in colonial and independent India. Devi also worked towards safeguarding the rights of indigenous communities and founded several organizations aimed at giving them access to education and healthcare and empowering them economically.

> "I HAVE SEEN THE STRUGGLES AND PROTESTS OF THE PEOPLE. FOR AN END TO THIS EXPLOITATION. FOR ACCESS TO BASICS WHICH ARE NEEDED FOR LIVING WITH DIGNITY. AND I FELT THAT I COULD NOT REMAIN A MERE WRITER OF FICTION WITHOUT DOING ANYTHING ABOUT IT."

13
CHAMPIONS OF SOCIAL JUSTICE

Vinoba Bhave (1895–1982) was a widely known and respected Gandhian reformer who began the Bhoodan movement in the 1950s. It was aimed at encouraging large landowners to redress historical wrongs by voluntarily giving up some of their land to the poor.

Poverty, illiteracy, and discrimination on the basis of gender, religion and caste are some of the most enduring challenges that India has faced in its long history.

For both the nationalist leaders and the Indian government after Independence, the need to confront historical discrimination and to find solutions to the social inequality it created shaped both the framing of the Indian constitution and the priorities of the Indian government in the first few decades after 1947.

However, alongside the government's efforts, there have always been individuals who have striven to create social change, often by dedicating their lives to specific causes.

You have already read briefly about the social and religious reformers of the nineteenth century, as well as women who founded women's rights organizations in colonial India and anti-caste activists who questioned and resisted the practices that had denied them human rights for centuries.

Many others have followed in their wake, often working in hostile conditions, facing social ostracism, and struggling with a lack of resources in the course of their work.
This section features a few of them: social activists and reformers whose work has brought succour to the many millions in distress in India.

MURLIDHAR DEVIDAS 'BABA' AMTE
1914–2008

> "I DON'T WANT TO BE A GREAT LEADER. I WANT TO BE A MAN WHO GOES AROUND WITH A LITTLE OIL CAN AND WHEN HE SEES A BREAKDOWN OFFERS HIS HELP. TO ME, THE MAN WHO DOES THAT IS GREATER THAN ANY HOLY MAN IN SAFFRON-COLOURED ROBES."

A conflicted life

Murlidhar Devidas Amte was born into a wealthy Brahmin landowning family in Warora, Maharashtra. Amte graduated with a law degree from Nagpur University in 1936 and set up a successful practice. He had long been uncomfortable with caste-based social segregation, poverty and income inequality, and this discomfort grew stronger as his career prospered. In 1940, he chose to return to his home district, to work towards social change and began organizing workers into unions, to try to improve their wages and working conditions. He also stood for election and took office as the vice-president of the Warora municipality, believing he could bring change by being part of local government. Inspired by Gandhi, he subsequently chose to renounce his wealth and live simply.

People with leprosy faced social stigma, and were often forced to live in isolation in poor conditions. Horrified by their plight, Amte was moved to study the disease, its symptoms and treatment protocols.

Love over fear

In the 1940s, Amte encountered a man suffering from the debilitating effects of leprosy, a disease that was thought to be highly contagious and was incurable at the time. In 1949, he set up the Maharogi Sewa Samiti (Leprosy Relief Society), and leased land from the government to set up a treatment and rehabilitation centre. This would come to be known as Anandwan, a village built and run by leprosy patients, where they engaged in agriculture and small-scale industrial production. Amte later set up several establishments and projects, including an orphanage, a home for the elderly, educational institutions and several communes and villages for the socially marginalized. In 1946, Amte fell in love with and married Sadhana (Indu) Guleshastri. The marriage was an unusual one at the time because it was not arranged by their parents. Sadhana worked closely with Amte in all his endeavours, beginning with their first attempt at creating an equitable community, Shram Ashram, soon after their wedding.

> In 1985, an ailing seventy-two-year-old Amte launched a bicycle rally from Kanyakumari to Kashmir, called the 'Bharat Jodo Yatra'. It was meant to encourage people to reject communal violence and promote national unity.

On the side of the dispossessed

In the 1970s, Amte founded the Lok Biradari Prakalp, an organization aimed at bringing healthcare and basic education to the Madia-Gond tribal community. Located in Gadchiroli district, Maharashtra, the Madia-Gonds lived in poverty and suffered from a variety of common illnesses caused by poor nutrition. Amte, along with his son and daughter-in-law, set up various institutions, including a hospital and a facility to teach the community agricultural techniques and basic reading, writing and arithmetic skills. Amte was also involved in protests against large hydroelectric projects (including those planned in the Narmada Valley) that would destroy forests and dispossess thousands of people of their land and homes. For his work through the years, which inspired many around the world, he received several honours and awards, including the Ramon Magsaysay award, the UN Human Rights prize, and the Gandhi Peace Prize.

In 1990, Amte left Anandwan to take part in the Narmada Bachao Andolan, and lived on the banks of the Narmada for seven years.

IN SERVICE OF HUMANITY

This section features four individuals whose brave, thoughtful and pioneering attempts to solve problems and help people in need made an impact in India and beyond.

ELA BHATT
1933–present

"POVERTY IS A FORM OF VIOLENCE; IT DOES NOT RESPECT HUMAN LABOUR, IT STRIPS A PERSON OF HUMANITY, AND IT TAKES AWAY THEIR FREEDOM."

Ela Bhatt was born in Ahmedabad. While working with the Textile Labour Association (TLA), one of the oldest labour unions in India, she learned of the difficulties faced by female informal workers, who did gruelling jobs for low pay with no job security. In 1972, Bhatt founded the Self-Employed Women's Association (SEWA) to help these workers demand better conditions and pay. Since then, SEWA has expanded to aid women in over a hundred other sectors, offering small loans for its members to start businesses; setting up cooperatives and benefit schemes, and helping its members share skills and knowledge. Bhatt has won awards and for her work with the Indian government and international organizations on issues such as poverty, safeguarding street vendors' livelihoods and encouraging women's self-employment and financial independence.

Ela Bhatt inspecting the handicrafts produced by the Kalandia Camp Women's Handicraft Cooperative, which was formed by nine Palestinian women.

Mabelle and **Rajanikant Arole** were a physician couple who founded the Comprehensive Rural Health Project (CRHP) to improve rural health in India. India's villages have historically suffered from a severe shortage of doctors. With this in mind, the Aroles pioneered a new method of helping people help each other. In 1970, they began the CRHP in Jamkhed, a poor, drought-stricken region of Maharashtra, to help people prevent minor ailments and diseases through better nutrition, access to clean water and education. The Aroles trained local women to observe symptoms, do simple tests and teach their peers about better hygiene and preventive measures against common diseases. As a result, health indicators in Jamkhed improved significantly. The project's success led to the Aroles' approach being adopted in dozens of countries across the world.

MABELLE AROLE
1935–1999

RAJANIKANT AROLE
1934–2011

> "...THE SOLUTION IS NOT TO BUILD A CLINIC, BUT TO CHANGE THE PEOPLE'S ATTITUDES TOWARDS WOMEN, CHILDREN, AND THE POOR."

Born in Madras, **Dr Suniti Solomon** was a pathologist and microbiologist. She is best-known for having identified the first cases of HIV in India in 1986. At the time, cases of HIV were rising all over the world, but the Indian government was unwilling to consider that the virus could have spread to India. Together with Sellappan Nirmala, a PhD student she was supervising, Solomon began a project to collect and test 100 local blood samples for HIV. The six positives they uncovered were concrete proof that the virus was already present in the population. Solomon subsequently shared her discovery with the government, enabling swift action to prevent the disease from spreading rapidly. Solomon herself spent the rest of her life championing affordable, compassionate care for those with HIV/AIDS, and fighting the social stigma surrounding the disease.

SUNITI SOLOMON
1939–2015

OTHER INCREDIBLE INDIANS

As is always the case with a book like this, many Indians who played a notable part in shaping India's history as a modern nation couldn't be included for lack of space. To address some of the gaps we had to leave, here is a small selection of other interesting Indians whose choices, beliefs and life's work left an impact on the nation at large. And if you're particularly intrigued by any of them, I would urge you to look them up, read about them, investigate their lives—and find out more about why they are special or important!

ANNA MANI

1918-2001

Pioneering scientist of the Indian Meteorological Department who helped design devices to more accurately measure aspects of the weather

ANNIE MASCARENE

1902-1964

Independence activist; political leader; member of the Constituent Assembly; first female Lok Sabha MP elected from Kerala

ARUNA ASAF ALI

1909–1996

Heroine of the independence movement; respected left-wing political figure and women's rights activist; first elected mayor of Delhi

AZIM HASHAM PREMJI

1945–present

Entrepreneur, philanthropist; founder chairman of the information technology firm Wipro Limited, one of the largest in the world

BANOO JEHANGIR COYAJI

1917–2004

Physician and founder of community-based rural healthcare projects, birth control and women's education programmes in Maharashtra

BIRBAL SAHNI

1891–1949

Palaeobotanist, distinguished academic and founder of the Birbal Sahni Institute of Paleobotany (Lucknow); pioneered the study of Indian plant fossils

CHAKRAVARTI RAJAGOPALACHARI

1878–1972

Independence activist; Congress member and writer; he founded the secular, right-wing Swatantra Party in 1959 after becoming dissatisfied with the Congress

DHUNDIRAJ GOVIND 'DADASAHEB' PHALKE

1870–1944

Pioneering film director, producer and scriptwriter; maker of India's first feature film in 1913, a silent movie named *Raja Harishchandra*

DHIRUBHAI AMBANI

1932–2002

Entrepreneur, giant of Indian business and founder of Reliance Industries, one of the world's largest corporations

DURGABAI DESHMUKH

1909–1981

Independence activist; member of the Constituent Assembly; social worker for women's welfare and education; founder of the Andhra Mahila Sabha (1938)

LAKSHMI SAHGAL

1914–2012

Physician; social worker and activist; member of SC Bose's Azad Hind government; commander of the women's regiment of the INA

LEILA SETH

1930–2017

Lawyer; first female judge of the Delhi High Court: first female chief justice of a state high court; champion of human rights and gender justice

MANMOHAN SINGH

1932–present

Economist; finance minister (1991–1996) who helped liberalize the Indian economy; prime minister of India (2004–2014); prioritized economic growth, education, rural healthcare and rural employment

PADMAVATHY BANDOPADHYAY

1944–present

Physician; researcher; specialist in aviation medicine; first female Air Marshal of the Indian Air Force

RAJ KAPOOR

1924–1988

Prolific and well-regarded actor, producer and director who made commercially successful films that highlighted social inequalities

RAJIV GANDHI

1944–1991

Prime minister of India (1984–1989) who further liberalized the Indian economy, enabling growth in the telecommunications and information technology industries

RAMNATH GOENKA

1904–1991

Member of the Constituent Assembly; MP; owned *The Indian Express* from 1936, a newspaper that persistently exposed political and bureaucratic corruption

RENUKA RAY

1904–1997

Member of the Constituent Assembly; West Bengal Legislature and Lok Sabha MP; women's rights activist, social worker and writer

RUKMINI DEVI ARUNDALE

1904–1986

Classical dancer remembered for popularizing Bharatanatyam in modern India and founding Kalakshetra, an academy dedicated to the study of the arts

SATYAJIT RAY

1921–1992

Internationally acclaimed filmmaker, scriptwriter, illustrator and writer whose films highlighted struggles modern Indians faced; he had a lasting influence on Indian cinema

SHEIKH MOHAMMAD ABDULLAH

1905–1982

Popular Kashmiri leader who founded the secular Jammu and Kashmir National Conference and negotiated for special status within India for the former princely state

SHRIPAD AMRIT DANGE

1899–1991

Lok Sabha MP; journalist; founding member of the Communist Party of India

TARA SINGH

1885–1967

Sikh political leader who advocated a separate state for Punjabi speakers, which led to the creation of Punjab in 1966

TN SESHAN

1932–2019

Chief election commissioner from 1990 to 1996, known for cracking down on corrupt practices and enforcing the model code of conduct

VK KRISHNA MENON

1896–1974

Independence activist; advocate for Indian independence in Britain; socialist; close political associate of Nehru; controversial defence minister of India (1957–62)

ABOUT THE AUTHOR

Ashwitha Jayakumar has loved stories all her life, especially ones set in different times and worlds. Born in Chennai, she studied English literature and medieval studies at the universities of Edinburgh and Leeds in the United Kingdom and has worked for over a decade in the Indian publishing industry. Her work has been published by Pratham Storyweaver, Scholastic India, Puffin Books and Hachette India. She particularly enjoys writing about history, a subject she has always been especially fond of.

ABOUT THE DESIGNER

Sergio Mario Studio is a Pune-based design studio that works across the area of children's media including comics, picture books, reference books and digital platforms. They have been working in collaboration with authors and other designers; and have worked with creative places like Amar Chitra Katha, HarperCollins India, *Tinkle*, Scholastic, *Sakal*, *National Geographic Traveller*, *The Hindu*, Jyotsna Prakashan, Mehta Publication, Dinardo Design to name a few.

ACKNOWLEDGEMENTS

The author would like to acknowledge the following works for enriching her perspective during the making of this book. Apart from these, she also consulted numerous newspaper articles, journal articles and other publications

On Indian history
Chandra, Bipan; Mukherjee, Mridula; Mukherjee, Aditya. *India Since Independence.* Penguin Books, 1999
Guha, Ramachandra. *India after Gandhi: The History of the World's Largest Democracy.* Picador, 2008
Khilnani, Sunil. *Ideas of India.* Penguin Books, 2012

Biographies
Personalities: A Comprehensive and Authentic Biographical Dictionary of Men who Matter in India [Northern India and Parliament], 1950
Basu, Narayani. *VP: The Unsung Architect of Modern India.* Simon & Schuster, 2020
Bose, Sugata. *His Majesty's Opponent: Subhas Chandra Bose and India's Struggle Against Empire.* Penguin India, 2013
Dhamija, Jasleen. *Kamaladevi Chattopadhyaya.* National Book Trust, India, 2007
Evans, Humphrey. *Thimayya of India.* Natraj Publishers, 2009
Frank, Katherine. *Indira: The Life of Indira Nehru Gandhi.* HarperCollins Publishers, 2001
Gandhi, Rajmohan. *Patel: A Life.* Navajivan Publishing House, 1991
Guha, Ramachandra,. *Makers of Modern India.* Viking, 2010
Guthrie, Anne, *Madame Ambassador*, Harcourt Brace, 1962
Kannan, R. *Anna: The Life and Times of C.N. Annadurai.* Penguin Books India, 2010
Kiro, Santosh, *The Life and Times of Jaipal Singh Munda.* Prabhat Prakashan, 2020
Khilnani, Sunil. *Incarnations: India in 50 Lives.* Allen Lane, 2016
Naravane, Vishwanath. S. *Sarojini Naidu: An Introduction to Her Life, Work, and Poetry.* Orient Longman, 1980
Natarajan, Srividya and S Anand. *Bhimayana.* Navayana Press. 2011
Paswan, Sanjay. *Encyclopedia of Dalits in India.* Kalpaz Publications, 2002
Shah, Amrita. *Vikram Sarabhai: A Life.* Penguin India, 2016
Singh, VK. *Leadership in the Indian Army: Biographies of Twelve Soldiers.* Sage Publications Pvt. Ltd, 2005
Sitapati, Vinay. *Jugalbandi: The BJP Before Modi.* Penguin Random House India, 2020
Sitapati, Vinay. *The Man Who Remade India.* Oxford University Press, 2018
Tharoor, Shashi. *Nehru: The Invention of India.* Penguin Random House India, 2003

Note to readers: These are largely books for adults and may not be appropriate for or accessible to children.

PICTURE CREDITS

HARPERCOLLINS WOULD LIKE TO THANK WIKIMEDIA COMMONS FOR REPRODUCING THE MATERIAL AVAILABLE ON THEIR WEBSITE.

(KEY: A-ABOVE; B-BELOW/BOTTOM; C-CENTRE; F-FAR; L-LEFT; R-RIGHT; T-TOP)

11 Wikipedia Commons: Jigar Brahmbhatt (CR); 13 Wikipedia Commons: Tyoron2; 15 Wikipedia Commons: Anonymousboii (CR); 21 Wikipedia Commons: India Post, Government of India (BR); 28 Wikipedia Commons: Reserve Bank of India (CR); 32 Wikipedia Commons: India Post, Government of India (TL); 35 Wikipedia Commons: India Post, Government of India (TL); 36 Photo Division, Govt. of India (TL); 37 Wikipedia Commons: Post of India; 38 Wikipedia Commons: Divinwrct (CR); 43 Wikipedia Commons: Indian Army (TL); 44 Wikipedia Commons: Indian Army (TL); 45 Wikipedia Commons: Fred the Oyster (CR); 46 Wikipedia Commons: Indian Navy(CL); 46 Wikipedia Commons: Additional Directorate General of Public Information, IHQ of MoD (Indian Army) (CR); 52 Wikipedia Commons: India Post, Government of India (TL); 53 Wikipedia Commons: User:Fotokannan (Kannanshanmugam) (BR); 54 Wikipedia Commons: India Post, Government of India (TL), Wikipedia Commons: Thamizhpparithi Maari (BL); 55 Wikipedia Commons: Zara2312 (BL); 61 Wikipedia Commons: Bhim Chandra Mondal (B); 63 Wikipedia Commons: 2006_Norman_Borlaug_Congressional_Gold_Medal_front (TR), India Post, Government of India (BR); 64 Wikipedia Commons: SubhranshuJi (TL); 64-65 Wikipedia Commons: Indian Space Research Organisation (B); 65 Wikipedia Commons: Bhaskar De (CR), James Stuby based on NASA image (BR); 66 Wikipedia Commons: Vinwe (BR); 73 Wikipedia Commons: Post of India (TL), Wikipedia Commons: Padmaxi (C), Wikipedia Commons: Pdpics (BR); 74 Wikipedia Commons: Nmgrandhi 1977 (CR); 79 Wikipedia Commons: Anefo (TL); 81 Wikipedia Commons: Oleg Yunakov (BR); 82 Wikipedia Commons: Vijae Goray (BR); 86 Wikipedia Commons: V. Santharam (TL), 87 Wikipedia Commons: Post of India (TL), Wikipedia Commons: Jaseem Hamza (B); 90 Wikipedia Commons: Kalpit Bishnoi (TL); 94 Ministry of External Affairs, India (TL), Wikipedia Commons: The Illustrated London News (BC); 95 Wikipedia Commons: Siddhesh Mangela (TR), Wikipedia Commons: Rogers Fund, 1928 (BL); 96 Wikipedia Commons: Ashish Bhatnagar (CR); 97 Wikipedia Commons: Post of India (CL), Wikipedia Commons: User:Midnightblueowl (BL); 98 Wikipedia Commons: Daderot; 101 Wikipedia Commons: Old Indian Photos (TL); 102 Wikipedia Commons: Howard Coster (TL), Wikipedia Commons: ANDMACRO (BR); 103 Wikipedia Commons: Polska Agencja Prasowa (C); 106 Wikipedia Commons: India Post, Government of India (BR); 109 Wikipedia Commons: India Post, Government of India (TL); 111 Wikipedia Commons: India Post, Government of India (TR), Wikipedia Commons: Supreet Patel (BL); 112 Wikipedia Commons: Wolfgang Holzem (TR), Wikipedia Commons: Haim Zach (BR)